Hopping
Seven
Continents

Kwang & Kooh-wha Koh

June, 2013

Hopping Seven Continents

Kwang and Kook-Wha Koh

Mountain Top Press
Northville, MI

Disclaimer

The author wishes to state that many of the names of the people in our travel groups are assumed names in order to protect their privacy. Also, some of the facts may be fictitious.

Published by
Mountain Top Press
Northville, MI

ISBN13: 978-0-9860327-0-7

LCCN: 2013930267

Printed in the United States of America
17 16 15 14 13 • 5 4 3 2 1

Dedication

This book is dedicated to the memory of my mother and especially to our family, our four children and their spouses and our grandchildren, Nicholas, Nathan, Soren, Gus, Erin, Patrick and Clare.

Contents

Acknowlegments

I deeply appreciate the help I received from the following people in the preparation of this book: First, Ms. Patti Goodwin (my secretary) typed this manuscript and continuously helped with the editing. My friend Dr. Agnes Moon and her friend Ms. Margaret Allen read the manuscript, did the first editing and offered me encouragement to publish the book. Also, I owe many thanks to Mr. John McCarthy and my friends in the Deadwood Writer's Club for their constructive criticism. My daughter Jung-Kyu and my friend Mr. Phil Rosette helped with the final editing. Finally, my husband Kwang took the pictures and designed the cover.

About the Authors

KWANG K. and **KOOK-WHA KOH** were both born in Korea and graduated from Seoul National University with Chemical Engineering degrees. They both obtained Ph.D.'s in Chemical Engineering from the University of Iowa.

Together they founded Chrysan Industries in 1977, manufacturing industrial lubricants and supplying the automotive industry. They officially retired from Chrysan in 2006.

Kwang and Kook-Wha remain as chairman and vice chairman of the board at Chrysan. They are active in local professional societies, such as (STLE) Society of Tribology and Lubrication Engineers and enjoy traveling.

This is their second book which consists of travel stories. *Across the 38th Parallel,* Kook-Wha's autobiography, was published in 2005.

ASIA

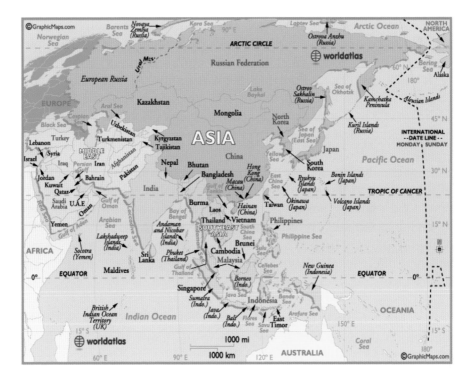

Mahjong

In October 2010, Kwang and I were on the Victoria Cruise Lines on the Yangtze River in China, from Chongqing, through the three gorges to the Three Gorges Dam in the Yiling District of Yichang, in Hubei province, China.

The ship was a small river boat which could handle only one hundred passengers and thirty crew members. Almost everywhere was occupied with guests. After a late dinner I was looking for a quiet place to write in my journal to avoid disturbing Kwang's early evening nap.

Usually the library was occupied by extra activities, with group discussions on politics and economic growth in China, especially after World War II, or sometimes lectures or calligraphy with black ink. Deck Four had a small room. Actually it is a game room next to the dining area. It was empty most of the time. *Ah, ah, it will be a nice place to spend a couple of hours,* I mumbled to myself and dashed to the fourth floor.

The door was closed. I did not see anybody on the north side of the room and thought the room was available. When I opened the door loud clicking sounds struck my eardrum and almost shattered it, and I automatically closed the door with a "Bang". The four Mahjong players looked at me without any interest in their intruder and bent their heads down again to collect the dice with their busy hands.

Oh, what a disappointment, again I mumbled to myself while leaning on the wall beside the door to the game room and planned my next step.

My disappointment was not only because the room was occupied, but also they were playing "Mahjong". Subconsciously all my life I have hated the people playing Mahjong which is an extremely intelligent game and excellent for passing the time. But I have always thought that playing Mahjong is gambling. I know I am not absolutely right, however it is true that this is how my feelings were running in my blood.

During World War II, I was still young but old enough that I could fret over on miserable memories about Mahjong from my great grandma or other relatives. At that time in Korea the above middle class people played Mahjong as an elite society game. One of my relatives lost his house and other belongings, and my great grandma told this story to relatives and her friends over and over again without anger or resentment. "He was really lucky that he did not lose his wife and extremely fortunate that he still has his important part as a man," she concluded with this sentence. In the beginning he played for fun, and to kill time during the long winter nights in North Korea, but later it became a big gamble, like an addiction to opium. He could not cut it off. After their harvest was gathered, from the beginning of winter to early spring, as a landowner he started to play Mahjong with a neighbor as a social game, but later without his notice, he was involved in a gambling society. Of course, he won and lost. After three winters, his land was gone and his house too. His two children and his wife moved into his elder brother's house where his grandma lived. As this thought filled my blood, I slowly took the steps towards our cabin on the second floor. *Umm. At least he did not sell his wife like a Chinese farmer,* again I mumbled to myself. I was told a Chinese farmer sold his wife after he lost playing the game Mahjong.

"Oh, you came back sooner than I expected." Kwang asked me if there was any reason. I threw my book on the bed without looking at him; he was busy too with his camera and trying to organize the pictures that he had taken over several days.

"I will take a very hot shower and sleep. I am too tired and cannot read a book or do anything," I told him while I was taking off my clothes. He did not ask me any more questions, without even looking at me, his hands were as busy as the Chinese Mahjong players. Suddenly, terrible exhaustion spread throughout my body, as though I had had a frightening nightmare last night.

The next day we had an excursion to the relocation village from Wu Gorge on the upper stream of the Yangtze River. The village was located about thirty minutes away by bus from Victoria line. It was on a beautiful scenic drive over a hill and looked down on the Yangtze River and the grandiose mountains were far away from the opposite side of the new location of the village, covered by clouds and fog.

A fairly new two-story cement building was spread out over three blocks on the street. One of the families where we visited has a convenience store at the bottom floor and the second floor is their living quarters. The store was about twenty five by thirty five feet, and had candies, ice cream bars, small rice bags, kitchen utensils, soap bars, toothpaste, almost everything for daily life. The next shop was a game room three or four Mahjong tables in a small space. Two tables were occupied by elderly men.

Now is the time I have to recalculate and organize my brain cells. I continued my mumbling. "Mahjong is not a game of gambling. It is like a chess game to pass and kill time for the Chinese seniors, and, I was told, has an unbelievable benefit for Alzheimer's or dementia." *Mahjong is a game and is not gambling.* I needed positive and constructive thinking to eliminate bad memories. Even with positive thoughts about Mahjong, Mahjong still is not my favorite game. Again I could see my mother's face serving snacks all night while rubbing her sleepy eyes for her grandfather who was playing Mahjong for a couple of days without sleeping or breaks except for rest room trips. "Let's only think about the positive side of the game," I told Kwang and myself. He could not understand what I meant but he did not ask me anything. He just showed me a curious face and shrugged his shoulders.

The next stop was a small market for the local people. Our group passed the meat and fish market which had pig heads with two big nose holes and chicken fingers, and the other stores had crops and kitchen aids with pots and pans and stainless steel rice bowls.

I saw a variety of Mahjong sets in the souvenir shop and also a Mahjong bracelet. Asking price was $15.00 each, with several lines negotiation I bought two bracelets for $15.00. I put them on my right arm immediately and thought about that.

4

About ten years ago, the first time we went to China we bought a Mahjong set as a souvenir for Kwang. One side with bamboo and other side is some animal bone (maybe elephant). Usually the dice are made of ivory but now most of them are plastic dice. "Kwang, they are playing Mahjong everywhere," finally I opened up my mind with concern and curiosity about the Mahjong culture in China. "Maybe it counts like chess or card games everywhere, everybody is playing," Kwang simply commented. "But a long time ago playing Mahjong in Korea was big time gambling," I answered back. "That was a long time ago," Kwang again asserted his opinion. "Women are playing too," was my comment. "Yes, women's liberation," Kwang answered without any interest.

A couple of months later after our China trip, the Wall Street Journal reported the spreading Mahjong game in the U.S., especially among young women in their thirties on the east coast of America just for playing games and social gatherings, and added that by playing Mahjong you can reduce the chance of getting Alzheimer's disease. *What a great benefit from playing Mahjong.* I read and read this sentence.

In the future I hope that wearing my bracelets and favorable reports on Mahjong will eliminate my unnecessary bad images of it, however, I do not have any intention of playing it.

Figure 1 Mahjong Play

Figure 2 Mahjong Players

Figure 3 Mahjong Set-

Potala Palace

Our Overseas Adventure Travel group totaled sixteen people from Florida, California, Michigan, Virginia, and the New York area, and we toured around China to Tibet.

Our tour guide in China, Mark, was about forty years old and had never been to the United States or England, but spoke fluent English with a Xian accent. He was medium sized and shaved his head like the actor, Yul Brynner. He always wore his shirt out from his pants to cover his round belly. The Potala Palace we were traveling to is located in Lhasa, Tibet, China. It is twelve thousand feet above sea level and the Uhuru peak in Kilimanjaro is about twenty thousand feet. Most tourists arrive here by train from Xian, spending a couple of days on the train adjusting to the altitude, but our group came here by airplane last night.

Yesterday, when we stopped at a field on the way to Lhasa from the airport, we saw a special species of "Yak", an animal somewhere between a cow and ox, and has long, thick hair covering its legs. When I stepped down from the bus, I felt a little dizzy and could not follow our group and returned to the bus and rested for a while with Mark who was having the same altitude problems.

It was quite chilly in the hotel lobby and the dining room during breakfast. But in our excitement we didn't mind. A friend, Innet, sat beside me and said, "Kook-Wha, for you it is a piece of cake to climb so many steps to the palace". I replied vaguely, "I hope so". I could not understand the reason she made such a comment. Maybe I am slimmer than she is or more active than other people. Anyway, the comment did not irritate me. Then we finished our simple breakfast of boiled eggs with fried noodles and headed for the bus.

Even though I had taken Diamox to fight the effects of altitude yesterday, my head was spinning and not clear this morning. Walking a short distance made me dizzy. I trailed slowly behind our group, talking to myself. *I have to see the Potala Palace. I cannot give up.* I tightly fisted my hands. *I made Kilimanjaro, so why can't*

I do this? My chest was getting tight and my dizziness did not go away. I took the steps one by one, slowly adjusting to the altitude.

Kwang was stubborn. He did not bring "Diamox", even though we had Diamox left over from our Kilimanjaro trip at home and I asked him a couple of times, "Kwang, did you take care of Diamox?" Flatly he said, "We do not need it, it is only twelve thousand feet." He continued, "And its height is almost the same as Machu Picchu. We climbed there without Diamox, so why do we need it?" His answer was a strong refusal and, with that sort of logic, I did not want to ask him about Diamox.

Along with my concern about the adjustment to the altitude, my right knee which has arthritis started to give me difficulty. I also noticed Kwang was starting to have problems too. "Kwang, are you okay?" I asked him, but I already knew his answer.

"No problem. I am fine." However, I noticed he lost his appetite this morning, like Mark, and he was sniffling. "Kwang, Marlene gave us enough Diamox and it's not too late to begin taking it." "I said I am fine," was his grumpy answer and he indicated that he would not change his mind by any means. "Okay. Okay. It's your problem if you get sick". I almost wanted to punch his face, I was so upset by his stubbornness.

Most of the people in Tibet have darker skin color, and thick pitch-black hair with an oily texture. Both men and women wear dark colored clothes. Women especially wore dark colored long skirts with coats or sweaters, and wore small aprons at their waist, which were the same rainbow striped pattern and the same colors for everybody. It was rare to see a young woman wearing jeans and jacket with high heels.

"Most of the women wear almost the same aprons, even on the street," I commented curiously to Mark. "It's a symbol of a married woman," Mark answered my comment with his hand on his forehead. I thought this was a very practical and simple tradition, using an apron for the symbol of marriage instead of wearing expensive rings.

Mark was sick from the altitude and the cold since yesterday. He was vomiting and could not eat any food. He looked really miserable and his face was turning a darker shade of green. He did not take any medicine. He was as stubborn as Kwang.

About a twenty minutes ride from the hotel we saw two or three storied old buildings which needed plenty of repairs and upgrading on the way to the Potala Palace. The first floors were stores for daily necessities and souvenir shops. Upstairs was living quarters. Among the stores, there were three - four guests who were having bowls of noodles at small local restaurants.

We all wore layers of clothes, because in the morning the temperature was down to 50 °F, and during the day it went up to 70 °F with plenty of sunshine. Our local guide, Denver, led us to the Potala Palace. The bus dropped us at two lane streets on each side and it was blocked with round rocks to prohibit passing automobiles on the street near the palace. The wave of local people heading to the palace for worship was similar to the pilgrimage to Mecca. Most of them were older people, walking with canes or supported by younger people who were holding their arms. Some had spinning wheels in their hand and were spinning in the air while they were walking. Surprisingly, I did not know the spinning mechanism, but I am sure it was very simple. It was fun to watch them as they spun, as if they were playing with them. "Denver, why doesn't everybody have a spinning wheel?" I asked. Denver gave me a quick answer and rushed to get our group together without losing our family in the wave of people. He was always more concerned about losing people from our group than about answering questions. Mark named our group "Mark's family," Denver just used it for his convenience. "Mark's family, let's stick together like sticky rice. Our assigned time inside the Potala Palace is 9 a.m. – 11:00 a.m. We have to keep to the timetable." We walked faster and we approached the grounds of the palace. The huge building loomed ahead. My dizziness was almost gone, from the Diamox, or my determination that I could not miss the tour.

We passed the first security checkpoint and came out in a small courtyard that had a couple of trees.

Mark warned us about making the decision to climb the steps. "If anybody cannot manage climbing about four hundred steps, stay with me under these trees," Mark continued, "Whoever can do it, follow Denver. This is your last chance to make your decision. There are a couple of more checkpoints inside, and once you pass these checkpoints there is no way you can come back to this point." To my surprise, nobody dropped out. We all decided to go ahead.

"Fantastic. Nobody will stay with me," Mark commented. We started to proceed climbing the steps, one by one. Kwang and I followed Denver, to listen to his explanations. If you are far away from the group, you might feel more tired from the psychology of being behind. We stopped at rest spots three times while climbing the four hundred steps.

Denver finally answered my question, "Some people feel spinning wheels show deep devotion to Buddha. Another method is counting beads in their hands to wash off their sins while praying to Buddha for wishes."

"Thank you," was my short answer. Then I saw the local people had beads in their hands and I hoped their wishes were achieved by counting beads and the spinning wheels. There were a thousand different types of spinning wheels, small, big, with bronze and silver, with semi-precious gemstone decorations. Most had long sticks for holding and the top of the stick had a spinning wheel positioned.

It was not easy ascending four hundred uneven stone stairs with zigzags higher up, at that altitude, and I climbed by touching the thick white stone walls between the stairs, for support, to prevent myself from falling. The white and red building of the Potala Palace was nearer. The thirteen-story white building was beautiful, elegant, and magnificent ancient Tibetan architecture of the seventh and seventeenth century.

"The outside is a stunning and beautiful white and red palace. It is really special ancient Tibetan architecture," Denver continued at the last resting area, moving his shoulders up and down, showing his pride in the palace and continued, "But you will be more amazed with the treasures inside. He paused before we moved on and warned again, "Stick together, Mark's family. If you get lost it will be very difficult to find us. Please stick together." He counted our group again and to make sure we were all there.

"Inside it is not easy to explain all the history and treasures. So, let me describe the history of the Potala Palace's construction before we start the tour inside". Denver's excitement about the history of the white and red Potala Palace, designated as a World Heritage Site by UNESCO in 1994, was never ending.

He continued, "The Great Fifth Dalai Lama started construction in 1645 after one of his advisers pointed out that the site was ideal, based on old superstitions. Construction continued until 1694, after his death. It has been used as a winter palace since that time, but was slightly damaged during the uprising in 1959, and it escaped more damage during the Cultural Revolution in 1966 through Chou En Lai's intervention." He continued with some excitement. He could talk about the palace for days and nights without tiring.

"Until the Fourteenth Dalai Lama fled to Bomdila, India in 1959, the White Palace was his residence. The lower stories were used as offices. Now the Chinese government has designated it as a museum and is using it as a government office." He had to stop because it was our group's turn to go inside the chambers.

The first place we visited was the Fourteenth Dalai Lama's residence where he had study, prayer and reception rooms, full of small and large statues of Buddha and colorful paintings on the poles, and the ceiling was covered with green, red, blue, yellow and white colors. Denver spoke in whispers with respect, "Blue means the sky, yellow is the earth, red is for fire, green is for trees, white for water".

Passing through narrow winding corridors, each room has Buddha statues and shrines with fifty - one hundred candles burning in about two foot diameter and one and one-half foot. deep stone or steel pots, and one-half foot. high, by two feet long, by one and one-half feet wide scent burners were in the corner of the chambers. Denver mentioned, "Before we used to use wax candles, but now we use vegetable oil in order to reduce the smoke inside. There was a reduction in tour hours, only 9 a.m. – 4:00 p.m., It helps to decrease the amount of smoke inside the chambers substantially. Maybe the smell of scent also is objectionable to certain people". Then without listening to our comments or opinions about the scent, he moved on to other chambers. Some local people worshipped with their hands together and their foreheads touching the screen that was made for the protection of Buddha and other statues. I was told there are more than ten thousand statues of copper, bronze and gold gild Buddhas or statues, and more than one thousand rooms in the Potala Palace. We passed statues from the Fifth Dalai Lama to the Thirteenth one.

Joe from Oregon asked quietly, "Hey, Denver, how do you choose the Dalai Lama?" and who will be the fifteenth one?" Denver answered, "It's complicated to answer now, I will explain it at lunch time." Joe did not consider this a satisfactory answer and was not a happy camper.

I asked Denver, "The Fourteenth Dalai Lama cannot come back to Tibet and the Fifteenth one has not been selected?" Again without answering we were moving into the next chambers and next, I already forgot what I saw. So many statues of Buddha and shrines in the chambers that all looked alike, but I hope they will protect us from evil and provide for our infinite happiness in our afterlife.

One interesting thing was one chamber has past, present and future Buddha statues which were in different sitting positions and the different gestures of the hands. I whispered to Kwang, "I never heard about Buddha, the past, present and future". He nudged my left side, "No, it is the first time for me, too". Then he put his finger to his mouth, warning me, "No more talk". Another odd thing was the Mandalas which is the palace in Heaven where the Dalai Lama could live after death (imaginary place) and had model building and gardens which is surrounded by different animals: snakes, elephants, tigers and others.

The most interesting chamber was the tombs of the Dalai Lamas, from the Fifth to the Thirteenth, generally forty to fifty ft. high, ten to fifteen feet wide, and made of sandalwood and solid gold, eight thousand to ten thousand pounds`` and decorated with one thousand different precious metals, diamonds, jade, turquoise, coral and others, with bottle shapes at the main body structure with the Dalai Lama's mummified body inside and usually four steps were supporting the structure of the stupa. Most of the tombs are in the red palace which was built in the seventh century and some portions of the white palace, built in the seventh century too, but most of them were destroyed and rebuilt in the seventeenth century. I regret I did not ask whether the bodies were still inside the tomb. This funeral service for the Dalai Lama was quite contradictory to that of ordinary people. Yesterday Denver explained to us on the bus from the airport to Lhasa about the unique funeral services in Tibet.

He told us the story of their funeral traditions. "The dead body is put in the field, sprayed with a special scent over it to coax vultures to eat the flesh, and when only the bones are left, they grind the bones and spray them in the field. Another funeral method is to put the body into the river with heavy rocks attached to weigh it down and then the fish eat the flesh". Everybody was quiet. We were not sure whether we wanted to hear more or not, but Denver continued, "The Tibetan people do not eat fish, but nowadays the younger generation have come back from abroad and they have started to eat fish, but not many," he concluded. Everybody was quiet because of the shocking tradition of the unique Tibetan funeral.

This story was from Denver just yesterday. But when I saw the stupas of the Dalai Lamas, *What a difference from the treatment of the ordinary people and the Dalai Lama!! It is not fair*. I sighed deeply. In Tibet the people respect the Dalai Lama, who is a combination of king and god. He is their spiritual and temporal ruler and leader. That is why he was treated quite differently from the ordinary Tibetan people. I was quite upset about the stupas. Denver added, ninety five percent of the Tibetan people believe in Buddhism. Five percent is a combination of Islam, Christianity and others".

Again Denver talked to us in whispers, "The last treasure, but not the least is the beautiful thangka (paintings on cloth) on silk or cotton was unique in Tibet. Another one is "yak" carpet or wool clothes from "yak fur".

There were so many statues and shrines of Buddha, Dalai Lamas, candle lights, and stupas and thangkas, it seemed that I could not remember anything. When we came out from the palace two hours later, the cloudless blue azure sky welcomed us, and with a nice breeze blew away the strong scent of the burning candles in vegetable oil. It was warm and quite comfortable weather without a jacket

We came out the back door of the palace which had one-half of the number of stairs as the front of the palace. When I looked over the palace again from the back, it was absolutely stunning architecture from the seventh century in Tibet.

On the way to lunch Denver could not hide his joy that he showed us the most magnificent treasures in Tibet. "How is it, Mark's family?" We all shouted with clapping, "Awesome." as we all took more pictures.

At lunchtime everybody had a "yak" hamburger, the famous Tibetan beef, with big fat French fries and small pickles.

My dizziness seemed to be almost gone because the Diamox was working, or because of the spectacular Potala Palace. I was so happy that I could see the fabulous and unique architecture in Tibet but Kwang's cold was getting worse. I forced him to take Tylenol. He could not refuse this time. "Our group will kick you out if you are coughing and sniffing your nose," was my strong order while giving him two tablets of Tylenol under the table.

Denver came to our table. "How is your "Yak" hamburger?" Of course, as he expected, we all said "Excellent". "By the way, the night view of the Potala Palace is something. You cannot miss it". He continued, "Take a rickshaw round trip. ¥10 is enough. It is a little far for walking distance," and continued, "You will have the experience of riding in a rickshaw and a spectacular night view of the palace".

Bob and Patricia from California and Joey and Effie from Washington, D. C. joined us for a night adventure to the Potala Palace. When we arrived at the square in front of the palace, it was about ten minutes before 8:00 p.m. The chilly air surrounded us after sunset. The palace at dusk was also spectacularly magnificent anchored to the mountain. After 8:00 p.m. the palace was lit. The white and red palace was a jewel of the Tibetan people.

Bathed in light, the palace stood wrapped in classical and jazz music, making the night seem alive. We left the square and the beautiful palace and returned to our hotel in a rickshaw crowded in the busy traffic of cars, motorcycles and more rickshaws.

Figure 4 Potala Palac

Figure 5 In front of Potala Palace

Figure 6 Scenery from Palace

The Three Gorges Dam

In order to tour the Three Gorges Dam we chose the Queen Victoria Cruise on the Yangtze River for three nights and four days between Chongqing and Yichang where the dam is located.

Between these two locations on the Yangtze River, the famous gorges, Qutang, Wu and Xiling are located on the route to the Three Gorges Dam. It was a brilliant idea to first write about the magnificent three gorges before the Three Gorges Dam in order to understand why the dam was built at Xiling Gorge near Yichang City.

We had an early buffet lunch on the ship, and at noon we disembarked and transferred to a small ferryboat which had glass windows and two decks in order to observe the gorges on the Yangtze River. The Chinese call it the "Changjiang River" (It means "long river" in Chinese) near Chongqing, but from Yichang to Shanghai it is called the Yangtze River. Foreigners know the whole water way as the Yangtze River.

Mark, the Overseas Adventure Travel China guide, advised us to "Bring a camera, or if you have binoculars, please bring them," he paused and then mentioned, "By the way, happy rooms are on the ferry". It was rainy, unusually chilly and cold. "You will need rain gear," he concluded.

The restroom facilities are different in each country, especially in China, when traveling outside of the USA. Most rural areas are still old style, just a hole without running water, and so-called "clean facilities" are not readily available. In the morning, with a cup of coffee, there is an increased need for frequency of trips to visit the restrooms for old folks like us. Mark nicknamed the restrooms "Happy rooms". For women, the happy rooms are the most important facility.

As soon as we were on the ferry, the first gorge, Qutang, from Changjiang River started near Chongqing City. Most of us sat near the windows to catch the spectacular scenery. Joe from Oregon, Kwang and a couple of other people were on the deck outside of the boat with umbrellas in order to enjoy a Kodak moment with the magnificent scenery. Kwang took out a telephoto lens and caught the mystic, cloudy, foggy mountaintop. "Over there, Kwang, the cloudy mountaintop. Take a picture, please. It seems to tell us ancient Chinese legends and unrevealed stories." I told Kwang, "I already did. There are so many beautiful peaks and strange rock formations, I do not know which one I should take". Kwang mumbled. "Yes. Too many," was my short response. "Look, Kook-Wha, the rocky wall from the bottom of the river to the sky," Ina from California added. About one hundred yards wide and maybe one hundred – two hundred yards high, the pinkish rock looked like a huge playground hung on the sky above the river. If it hadn't been so foggy, I might have been able to guess the peak's height. Joe was still on the deck shivering. I could see his shoulders getting smaller and smaller and his cap was soaked by raindrops.

The river was zigzagging with layers of mountain, and still the top of the mountain was covered with white, gray clouds among the dense fog. All of us were quiet, trying to absorb the splendor and stunning natural powers. I saw fjords in Norway, Australia and New Zealand, but this is the first time I had witnessed fjords on such a grandiose scale and mystery of natural wonders.

According to the rule or law of tourism in China, we have to hire a local guide in each city we visited. The local guide, Nick, also on the ferry, explained it spot by spot, the rock formations and special trees. Nick was slender, short, wearing black pants, and a black shirt with a crew cut. He started to explain, "In the gorge, the most spectacular thing is the hanging coffins".

We were told before about the hanging coffins by Mark, so we were not surprised, nor were we interested. The local guide was excited and continued, "In five to seven minutes we can see a hanging coffins in the middle of the mountain. Actually on the middle of the rock wall to your left," he continued, "The coffin is about two thousand years old. It is still inside the cave". "Wow, wow," Joe and Ina exclaimed together. Kwang and I rushed out to the deck after he changed his camera to the telephoto lens.

The coffin was in the middle of the mountain, gray-reddish rocky surface, and had two holes (maybe caves). One is rather larger compared to the other when viewed side by side. Inside the large cave, I could see with my naked eye a black object. The image was unclear, but I tried to catch it with my camera without a telephoto lens. "Your camera cannot catch the picture," Kwang said as a friendly reminder. "Kwang, I know," I said. My voice was an octave higher than normal, indicating that I did not need his reminder, nor did I need any more lessons on how to take a picture with the camera, Canon EOS 20D, which he had handed down to me when he got a new Canon EOS 5D with a very expensive telephoto lens.

Of course, with his camera the image came out clearly. Marlene from Oregon took a picture with her small digital Lumix DMC-7S7.

Kwang wanted to show his complicated, advanced camera to everybody and was proud of himself for his superior skill in taking pictures, especially to me. I mumbled to myself, *Kwang, your skill is not good enough like Marlene's. She took nice pictures of the coffins from far away, without a telephoto lens and with a small digital camera.* I did not say this out loud, because he took pictures under a heavy rain and I did not want to discourage him.

I could not understand how the coffin remained for two thousand years in all kinds of weather, damp, rainy, foggy, cold and heat. If the location was Egypt, "yes" I could understand. Dry weather and no humidity can preserve many valuable objects for several thousand years, but not this Qutang Gorge. If the coffin is made of wood, what kind of protective coating did they used to use, and steel, too? Is the natural preservative tung oil product which has been used for a thousand years? This would make a very interesting research project for coating industries.

It made me think of the lubricant industry studying the fundamental causes of rust and development of theory and rust preventives. But I never heard about a product that could last two thousand years. We have to investigate the fundamental differences between modern technology and the ancient Chinese.

As we continued, the gorge was getting narrow, so we transferred to a pontoon boat for about a thirty minute ride. The boat's roof was made with banana leaves on a plastic sheet. The operator also had a banana leaf raincoat and hat.

Through Qutang, we came to the next gorge, which was Wu Gorge, with almost the same geographical structure, but one difference was that we could see the old tracker road. Now it is much lower than before, much closer to the river surface. When I saw the tracker road, it reminded me that naked men pulled the boat at the shallow river with a rope on their shoulders before the river's level is higher than before. This picture was shown at the "Queen Victoria" by Aaron, the ship moderator. "Kwang, do you remember the slide from Aaron from the ship?" I asked him. "Yes. I think around here they did, when the stream was shallow," Kwang shivered from the chilly wind. "Do you remember why they were naked?" "No," he answered grumpily, putting his hands in his coat pockets.

"Aaron told us the reason, or he does not know the reason why they were naked?" I asked him again. "No," he answered, indicating no more questions. "I am cold, Kook-Wha," he added, showing no interest in any questions. "When I go back to our ship I will ask him," I added in an unpleasant mood. It does not matter that we know the reason, but it is an interesting story.

The rain did not stop, but turned into much smaller drops. The clouds hanging on the top of the mountain were the same and the mountain was covered with rocks, and the green trees spreading on the river were the same as the Qutang Gorge.

Wu Gorge, about forty five kilometers long, and the famous twelve mysterious peaks still show us elegance and tell us beautiful stories. We were inside for a few minutes to get warm. The local guide told us about five to ten minutes later we could see the famous peak "on your left". No exception, Kwang and I rushed out to the deck and the camera was ready, but nothing came out at the special peak. "Kwang, did you see it?" He shook his head and did not say anything, but was ready with the camera posed. Later he told me, "We missed it". "I think so, because of the clouds, we could not see anything," I agreed with him, and with great disappointment I was speechless. It was a puzzle to me. "Are the Qutang and Wu Gorges area always foggy and the clouds covering the top of the mountain? Or does the sun show up on any special day?"

The next morning we arrived at Xiling Gorge where the hydro dam is located. The rain stopped, but it was windy, a strong wind even blew away the plastic lawn chair. At 11:00 a.m., Aaron again narrated the Xiling Gorge story. We were inside the cruise ship and passing beautiful cliffs and falls.

"My favorite bridge is on your left," Aaron started to narrate. Again, even against the strong wind, almost everybody was out on the fourth floor deck, including, of course, Joe, Jorge and Kwang. Aaron continued, "It is called McDonald Bridge. It looks like the McDonald's golden arch. Local kids like to play "hide and seek" on the bridge". When the ship approached, the red bridge looked like a zigzag shape. The ship cruised smoothly against the strong wind, so we all went inside again to warm ourselves up.

"Another bridge is coming up. It is the oldest, natural bridge in the world," Aaron was excited again about the bridge, as if it was his own treasure. "On your left at eleven o'clock, look at it, do not miss a picture". People were confused about finding it. "In the middle of the mountain there are big holes, there is a bridge," Aaron continued.

I saw the hole but could not spot the bridge. However, I took a picture of the hole as a bridge anyway.

A few minutes passed and everybody wished the clouds around the mountaintop would dissipate, since the dense fog was lifting up a little and, hopefully, we could see sunshine.

Aaron again, "In five or ten minutes on your right, Dragon Beach is coming. This is the place I like most. In the summertime you can swim here and go hiking in the mountains".

Ron from California commented doubtfully, "With this cliff and wall of rocks and green trees hanging on like a drapery, where can we find the beach?" Aaron continued, ignoring Ron, "After the small black tea house, there will be a small beach where people swim in the summer".

Everybody was quiet because we could not believe any beach could exist in this gorge. To our surprise, there was a small farmhouse and again, much smaller houses with black roofs, then also a running stream coming out from the valley like small falls and I could see the small white sand beach beside three or four pontoon boats waiting for guests. "Wow. Wow," everybody made noise at one time.

A few minutes later, again Aaron announced, "It's time to have a quick lunch and have an excursion for the Three Gorges Dam," and continued, "As you can see, Xiling Gorge is almost over. Now we have to see the magnificent engineering masterpiece of the world, the Three Gorges Dam".

After lunch we disembarked from the ship and went to the observation area at the Three Gorges Dam by bus, after a series of security checks. The local guide here was Wendy. She said, "OAT Group, please stick together, otherwise you will miss the bus and then you will miss the ship". She continued, "Stick together like sticky rice and I will give you free time for a Kodak moment". Francis from California and of course Kwang, were busy taking pictures because they were afraid of missing the best location and the best time for pictures. Wendy was small with long shiny black hair in a ponytail. She explained the history of dam construction and its benefits and drawbacks. Everyone was sticking together but our minds were on the monstrous dam, not her voice.

Interrupted by Wendy's voice again, we listened to her commentary. "In 1919, Dr. Sun Yat Sen proposed the dam project to the government but the proposal did not go through". After a while she asked, "Who played the pivotal role for this project to proceed?" That regained our attention.

"Mao Tse Tung," Ron from Florida gave her the right answer. Ron made notes like me and read the tour guidebook, studying diligently for this trip. He is a mechanical engineer, still working part-time as a consultant for heating and cooling systems. It reminded me of the famous poem from Mao Tse Tung, who was a great swimmer, "Swimming" on the Yangtze River.

She continued to explain, "It will take five minutes to explain the Three Gorges Dam and then I will give you free time to take pictures". She was begging for our attention and then spreading the two meters long map, unfolded one by one, she explained the location and size of the dam. The Three Gorges Dam is located in Zhongbao Island of Sandouping in Yichang City where the last gorge, Xiling, ended. "Just remember the dam is in Yichang City and 1.4 miles long, one hundred eighty five meters high, thirty two turbines and five steps ship locks". "The average water height is one hundred seventy five meters in summer and in winter the height is about one hundred forty five meters". She explained the chronological history about the dam construction. "But even though the dam was constructed under the budget of thirty billion dollars, in 2008 we had a problem in ship lifting. It will be done right, in the correct way by 2015". Ron and Joe asked at the same time, "How will the design be changed?" "From hydraulic lift to chain lift system," she answered. "Wendy, where did the Chinese government get the financial support for the Three Gorges Dam?" I asked.

"Good question." She started to state more about the financial structure and technology development for the project. The financial support from several sources: the Chinese Construction Bank, the profit of the Gezhouba Dam and foreign investments, but she proudly told us, "Most of the money came from the Chinese government and the Chinese Construction Bank. The technical transfer and design help came from Voith, General Electric, Siemens (VGS) and German companies. Now, let's discuss concerns before or after the Three Gorges Dam was constructed".

I thought this was a waste of time. We heard these comments from Mark and Aaron. She cited, "The concerns were relocations for one million three hundred thousand people. From farm land, environmental concerns, land erosion and silt problems," and continued, "but all the problems are almost solved. The one million three hundred thousand relocated people are happy with their new life from old style farmers," and she did not stop talking. "The saddest things were that the pink cranes and the Yangtze River dolphins are gone since the dam was constructed".

Now Wendy could not collect all the attention anymore. She gave us free time and told us our meeting point.

Kwang and I went to the highest point of the hill near the Three Gorges Dam and looked down at the huge, magnificent dam. This is one of the greatest human challenges against the power of nature. How far can we challenge the power of nature? Myself, as an engineer and scientist, I was astonished at the greatest technological achievement in the world, the Three Gorges Dam.

Figure 7 Three Gorge

Figure 8 Three Gorge Dam

Figure 9 Three Gorge Dam

Figure 10 Three Gorge Dam

Figure 11 Bridge across Three Gorge

Figure 12 Along Three Gorge

Figure 13 Dragon Beach in Three Gorge

Figure 14 Sailing along Three Gorge

Yi Xian Family

In October 2010, Kwang and I had a chance to tour the southern part of China with the Overseas Adventure Travel Tour Company (OAT) for three weeks through Shanghai, Beijing, Xian and other locations.

OAT included the program "Cultural Interaction with Local People", such as visiting local families, having lunch with them, or sleeping overnight. Today is the day for the sixteen people in our group to stay overnight at the farmhouse.

After lunch at a local restaurant in Xian, we were so excited about visiting a peasant village and having a sleepover with a Chinese family in Hu Xian, about forty miles away from Xian, for an exchange of cultural experiences. Mark held the microphone and spoke, "The hostesses are very nice and lovely people and will try to communicate with you even though they speak very little English." "Will we sleep over?" Effie from Washington D. C. questioned, implying her concern about sleeping at somebody's house, especially in China, and moreover at a farmer's house. "Let me finish our schedule," Mark interrupted her and continued, "There will be two families in each house, for four units, and I will tell you later your hostess' names." Mark continued, "and also will tell you the step by step procedure when we arrive at the village".

Everyone was pondering, I would say rather, wondering "why did OAT put together this program?" Mark proudly told us this way we could experience the real Chinese culture rather than just visit museums and famous historical places.

Chinese peasant house. Yes. My recollection went beyond 65 years ago when I was growing up in Manchuria, China, when I was between five and eight years old. I had a tiny Chinese playmate, she came over to my house, and so did I to her house. I assume that her family was rich, not like coolies who brought water for us every day. Her house was in the middle of a cornfield and had big red wooden doors. After passing three to four doors, I finally went into the family quarters. I have no memory of what was between the doors. The big family and living room combination was on a dirt floor, two feet above the floor, and at the end of the living room, was a huge reddish brown coffin with a nice design for their grandfather. He was still alive but this was preparing for his funeral. There was no divider between the living room and kitchen. Every time I visited her house her mother was sewing and embroidering her small shoes. At that time Chinese women bound their feet and walked like ducks. I was told that the Chinese custom of binding women's feet began to prevent the women from running away from their husbands, and the walking style that resulted was beautiful in the eyes of Chinese men.

I was worried that we might share a bedroom with another couple and sleep on the floor and maybe the bathroom facilities might be outside of the house. *I do not want to think about it happening; if it happens, it happens. Kook-Wha, don't worry, you spent several nights in a tent in Patagonia, Argentina and the Serengeti in Tanzania,* I said to myself.

While my imagination was flying, the tour bus was already turning in the direction of the village from the main highway to a four-way street. Along the street, yellow corn, ears of corn, and in some areas small unripe barley corn were spread on the street in order to dry them under the October sun. It looked like a masterpiece by Vincent Van Gogh or a street scene by Pablo Picasso, with yellow color.

"Kwang, look at that, take a picture quick, quick," I told him, excited at the unique scene. "How can they do that? Kind of invading the territory of the streets, and look at the cars, they are slowing down to avoid crushing the corn".

While Kwang took several pictures through the window, I was still looking for a farmhouse. Mark held the microphone again, "Hello, folks, we are almost at the village of Dong Han. The direct translation is 'East Chinese Village'. When the bus stops please wait until I tell you each hostess' name."

The bus went through the arched gate. On the left hand side a big sign read "Dong Han Village" in Chinese. Inside the arch, the beautiful western style two story houses were landscaped with evergreen shrubs around the house.

This is a farmhouse? I murmured to myself, *or a vacation home?* I was really confused, almost shocked that the Chinese farmhouses gathered together looked like a small Bavarian village.

"This Dong Han Village is about ten years old and was relocated from the old village," Mark told us the history of the village.

"About ten years ago, under communism, how could farmers have money?" Joe from Oregon asked.

"Good question. Ten years ago the government and banks gave the farmers a ¥50,000 loan for a house (about $7,500.00 in U. S. Dollars) and the farmers finished the house from a skeleton. The houses the government built were very basic," Mark continued, "At the beginning, the farmers were reluctant to move for a couple of reasons. Some families did not have the workforce to finish the house, because only old folks were living there, and the second was that some people were lazy and the extra work was too difficult. That's why about 20 families are still in the old village. This new village has about 260 families and 1,000 family members."

The bus stopped and the four hostesses were waiting for us. Yi Xian greeted us with her two daughters-in-law at the bus. Bob and Patricia from California stayed in the same house with us. Yi Xian was about 50 years old and short, medium size with a dark complexion without any make-up with a long thin ponytail. "Ni hau". "Ni hau", exchanged greetings and immediately she took my luggage from my hand with a welcoming gesture. She wore a long sleeved T-shirt and very tight black pants. We passed the small alley in her back yard. The door was open but hung on the thick plastic striped curtain. She showed us our bedrooms. Two full size beds side by side divided by a very small end table and one corner of the room had a small drawer and two green armchairs were in our room. The slate bedroom floor was better than cement. Heavy red ruffled curtains hung in the window. There were no decorations on the wall at all. An advertisement pamphlet of liquor and one scroll of typical Chinese scenery were on the wall. The bathroom had a very tiny sink and between the toilet and the sink there was a showerhead without any curtains around. Two small gray hand towels hung on a hot water pipe. They were originally white or gray, I was not sure. The original design of the house was beautiful and practical, but due to lack of maintenance, it looked older than ten years.

Mark suggested strongly that we talk with our hostesses in order to understand cultural differences between the East and West, "Please, ladies and gentlemen, interact with them, such as cooking together and trying to communicate, even with little English and no Chinese". Mark regarded our OAT group as his family. After a cup of green tea, Yi Xian started to prepare dinner for us. Naturally our interaction started in the kitchen.

I put on Yi Xian's apron and took over her kitchen to cook our dinner. First, we made dough, and had to reduce the thickness of the dough and increase its diameter from five inches diameter to twenty four inches. I thought we would make dumplings, but on the thin dough, the oil (maybe corn) was spread over and one and one-half inch width cut it, like long wide spaghetti and piled up all together, make a thick dough again about twelve inch diameter and cooked in the fry pan. Later I cut it two inch by three inch to serve as dessert bread with a little sugar sprinkled on it. It was delicious. If I have time, I would like to make this for breakfast at home, replacing bagels.

The next dish was in a big wok on the electric stove. We poured a cup of oil, raised the temperature very high and added cauliflower and carrots that Yi Xian had already cut then quickly sauteed. Next, we scrambled eggs with sliced tomatoes. Again I put one cup of oil in the wok at a very high temperature and added five eggs, scrambled them quickly, and added sliced tomatoes over it. Finally, we shredded potatoes for another dish, cooked in the same wok.

The seasonings which they used included sugar, salt, black pepper, MSG and a little red pepper for a spicy taste. The difference in cooking between Yi Xian and myself was that she used only one wok for every dish except the bread and another one was using a cup of oil to make small dishes, and mine was a couple of tablespoons to saute.

Dinner was ready with the dishes we made. One dish Yi Xian prepared before our arrival was crepes for wrapping vegetables, potatoes and scrambled eggs, which we put inside the crepes and shoveled into our mouths.

The table was round for four people but six people sat on stools which were just big enough for my small butt. Yi Xian brought her grandson, one and one-half years old, just learning words, but to our surprise he could say "Thank you, thank you" with a Chinese accent and with a cute smile. Since we were all hungry, without any words, we quickly had a couple of crepes then we started conversation in a relaxed mood.

"Ding, Dinghola (very very good)". I started. "Shee, shee" (thank you, thank you) Yi Xian responded. With hands, fingers and body language, I could understand she has two daughters-in-law living together and another grandson older than the baby, seven or eight years old. Her husband is working as a salesman for a company.

We introduced ourselves but I do not know if Yi Xian understood that Bob was a retired computer engineer from Hewlett Packard, and Patricia was a nurse. At the end of dinner, Yi Xian's husband joined us. He brought a bowl of noodles, which was cooked in the same wok with a few vegetables, and diced tofu with lots of water. After the water boiled, he added the noodles with MSG. The noodles in a small bowl were the last dish. It was delicious.

For her husband (dressed in a suit with a white shirt, but no necktie) we could ask his name and job and others but could not communicate, just saying, "Ding ho la" or "Shee, shee". But a smile was our tool for communication. He stayed with us a couple of minutes and then left us with an excuse. It was too bad that we could not communicate well.

The kitchen had a tiled counter, one sink and on the opposite side of the tiled counter was a wooden table with multifunctional use, such as a cutting board, rolling dough and others. The small chiller for cooling food stood between two counters, which were much lower than for my height. Between the kitchen and the main building of the house, two motorcycles were parked. The kitchen was added by extension to make more room for the house. We came in the back door. There was a front entrance with a steel bar attached to the living room with one TV and one sofa and tea table. It had very little decorations. Upstairs there was a bathroom, two guest rooms and one more bedroom, which the grandma used (Yi Xian).

After dinner we got together at the community playground about one block away from Yi Xian's house. The loud music was vibrating all over the village. It was 7:30 p.m.

Past the small sidewalk with green evergreens on both sides was a playground with swing sets and seesaws. The loud music was coming from the left side wall and the ground had a cement floor with two basketball rings with a worn out net. A girl was playing basketball. I joined her and meanwhile, our OAT group joined the local young people who can speak a little English. Later, more local ladies joined including our hostess, Yi Xian, and we started to dance along with the music, the chicken dance, macarena, and other group dances. All the Chinese women, young or old, they were good dancers. After about one and one-half hours exercise we came to our hostess' house. Her grandson was still wide awake. He showed us the stairs to go upstairs to the bedrooms.

I could do nothing tonight. The light was dim and the bed was different than mine, of course, but it was not cold. Mosquitoes were around with "wang wang" over my head.

I covered my head with the blanket. A couple of times I woke up in the middle of the night. Around 4:30 a.m. Kwang and I got up and changed our clothes and were almost ready to go. Breakfast was at 7:00 a.m. We still had to wait almost three hours. Of course, the radio or TV was not in the room. There was absolutely nothing to do. I took out my Hilary Spurling book, "Road to China" and started to read under the dim light.

"Kook-Wha, be careful of your eyesight. The dim light is not good for your eyes," Kwang said with concern. "Yes, but nothing to do. I cannot go back to bed. We still have three hours to go". "Yes, Yi Xian takes foreign guests quite often," Kwang observed the eight by eleven inch white sheet on the wall near the door printed in

English and Chinese, such as "Welcome", "Good morning" and "Goodbye". "You try to sleep again. I will read the book. I am ok." I encouraged Kwang to go back to sleep.

At 7:00 a.m., Yi Xian knocked on the door for breakfast. Bob and Patricia also woke up a long time ago. They waited in their room. Yi Xian asked me again to help her in the kitchen. The same wok, put in a cup of oil, cauliflower, carrot mixture and sauteed and made one dish. Breakfast was boiled brown eggs, mixed vegetables, crepes stuffed with vegetables, homemade cookies with sweet soft texture and barley and small bean soup and wulong tea. A very simple breakfast but it was quite adequate.

Yi Xian told us with her hands and head, that the baby, her husband and two daughters-in-law were still sleeping. At the breakfast table, most of the time she was in and out supplying tea and other things. So we had a chance to talk with Patricia and Bob alone, asking basic, ordinary questions, such as the number of children, job before retirement.

Yi Xian came to the dining room and indicated that we had to go someplace. When we came out on the street, we were the last ones to join our group that were heading to the west, to an old farm village divided by a two way highway. As soon as we crossed the road, we were at Dong Han Village (West Village). It had run down houses and wild plants, some small areas had green onions, cabbage and squash vines were underground. Trash was everywhere, maybe better than some villages in India. We came to the cornfield where the collective farm site was. Each family has about two acres, very small land, compared to American style, which may have one thousand acres for farmers.

"Mark, the land seems quite small to harvest enough for family income," I asked.

"Right, so most families have a side job, such as Yi Xian's husband is a salesman, but some families have to live on the income from the harvest". "Mark, again, corn is a government assigned crop? Or farmers can choose their own one?" I interrupted him. "Before two years ago, the government restricted the crops and assigned the produce in the field, but it did not work well and the government changed the policy, no restrictions," Mark shrugged his shoulders and answered my question proudly. Immediately I thought, the Chinese are operating two systems for one direction, the government system is communist, but the economical one is capitalism where you may earn as much as you can.

Joyce from Washington, D. C. asked, "Hello, Mark, what about taxes? Do farmers pay taxes?" "No, the government eliminated taxes two years ago," Mark again answered the question. "Mark, are these kinds of projects all over China, or only this Dong Han Village?" I asked with great curiosity. "All over China", was his short answer.

We left the old west side farm village behind and came back to the new Dong Han Village for a bus ride to the airport to go to see the panda breeding grounds.

Two things we did not notice last night in this village, one was a small bar and restaurant in a residential area, and another was that around the house in the flowerbed they planted green onions, turnips, Chinese cabbage and other vegetables, behind the evergreen shrubs, like my mother did many years ago in the flowerbed.

Just staying overnight I could not catch many differences from the culture in China, but I noticed a couple of things. One is that Chinese women are not easily intimidated or shy anymore and are very open-minded. With the 'only one child' policy, they have more time to take care of themselves.

Figure 15   Drying Corn on the Streat

Figure 16 At Yi Xian's Kitchen

Figure 17 Making Dumpling

Southern India Trip

On Christmas Day, the Delta VIP lounge in Detroit was as busy as usual. We took the last table in the lounge. I scanned a couple of newspapers with coffee and made final calls to our sons and daughter to wish them all "Merry Christmas and Happy New Year" before our departure for India.

We all boarded the plane and were ready to depart. Thirty minutes and one hour was gone, but no clue for departure. After a short apology for the delay from the captain, the stewardess announced that they would soon be ready after the final security clearance. Everybody was wondering what kind of security check, but nobody dared to ask. Another one-half hour was gone and we were told again the security was not clear yet. After two more hours delay the Delta flight to Amsterdam finally left Detroit. Usually mechanical problems are one of the reasons for delaying departure, but strangely enough, the captain did not tell us about mechanical problems.

To my surprise, the connection from Amsterdam to Mumbai was extremely smooth despite the three-hour delay. It seemed the airplane to Mumbai was waiting for a particular airline from Detroit. Later we found out terrorists (Umar Farouk Abdul Mutallab) attacked the airplane from Amsterdam to Detroit on Christmas Day, causing the delay of departure.

At the Mumbai airport we already felt the heat wave and had to take off layers of clothes, coat, turtleneck and sweater and only wore light T-shirt in the heat – 80 - 85 $^{\circ}$F.

Without touring Mumbai, we flew out to Kochi, which was the starting point of our Southern India trip via a small domestic flight.

When we arrived at the hotel Casa de Fort in Kochi it was already noon on December 27, 2009. We had already spent two days traveling. "Bani" introduced himself as our guide for our fourteen day trip in southern India. The mosquitoes were flying around in the hotel lobby and I was already uncomfortable from sticky moisture with heat and mosquitoes.

Five states belong to southern India. We covered four states and cities from Kochi, Coonoor, Mudumalai, Mysore, Chennai, Mamallapuram, Tanjore, Madurai, Periyar, Alleppey and came back to Kochi through the State of Kerala for a fourteen day trip.

We saw a Kathakali show in Kochi, coffee and tea plantations, a tiger reserve park, Mysore Palace, Chamundi Hills, Somanathapura Temple, Shore Temple, French colony Pondicherry, Hindu temples in Brihadeshwara and Srirangam and Meenakshi and the Gandhi Museum. These were unforgettable memories, but among these, tea plantations, Mysore and Hindu temples and the Gandhi Museum made the most tremendous impression on me. Kerala is one of the 50 places to visit in your lifetime recommended by the National Geographic Magazine. Of course, Kerala is included in my writing.

I wrote here about several highlights and the unique experiences we had, such as a Chinese fishing net, Nilgiri tea, Mysore Palace, Gandhi Museum, Kerala Backwater, and Hindu temples.

To my surprise the first thing that I noticed at the Hotel of Case de Fort was the shining Christian symbol of a cross on the wall at the main lobby area. I thought Hindu dominated the country. Later I was told by Bani that the official record is thirty percent Christian in southern India, but the actual number should be higher. This could be right, because I saw many small Catholic churches on the streets.

On a huge rain tree in the park with a diameter of about thirty yards, there were thousands of small lights glittering like a Christmas tree; but contrary to this, private homes had one or two huge plastic stars with lights inside, like balloons, with one or two feet diameter. They hung atop the door or on the roof.

A. Chinese Fishing Net

On the first visit was the Chinese fishing net on the shore of the Arabian Sea. Between the fifteenth and the sixteenth century Chinese came here and left behind fishing technology which is still being used for the fishing industry. The nets look like upside down umbrellas of octagonal shape. They are not easy to describe but they look to me like about ten meters wide, five meters high black-netted butterflies. These nets are used sinking a net under the water and lifting it up full with fish. The fish on a small table covered by a blue plastic tablecloth were for sale. Even a small pile of shrimp and a couple of squid were on the table. I hope that the fish on the table were fresh under the hot heat. A couple of miles away big cargo boats were docked with products waiting to unload. It was quite a contrast: five hundred years old Chinese technology versus modern one.

Figure 18   Chinese Fishing Net

B. Nilgiri Tea

When we think of tea, we think about Chinese and Japanese green tea or English black tea and sometimes Ceylon tea which is the most mild tea. I was especially ignorant of the fact that India's production of tea is next to that of China.

The region of Tamil Nadu and Kerala in southern India are the main tea plantation areas in the blue mountain with a high altitude. Dense fog covers the middle of the mountain until late morning. When we drove to the blue mountain among the tea plantations the fog was still draped over the green tea plants and the panoramic scene of the western houses with painted basic colors (pink, purple and bright blue) were erupting among the fog and green tea fields. Nilgiri tea has the reputation of a rich fragrance and a strong liquor taste. Also, Bani told us Nilgiri is the greatest exporter of tea to the world, after Sri Lanka, Kenya and China

Bani told us that tea drinking started in China five thousand years ago. Shen Nung, who was a skilled ruler, creative scientist and patron of the arts, accidentally founded tea drinking.

Bani continued,

"Even though at the tea auctions Nilgiri tea had a reputation as "good or excellent", the rugged mountain limits its production and prohibits spreading Nilgiri tea to the world. The Darjeeling Himalayan Railway, nicknamed the "Toy Train", is a two foot (610 mm) narrow-gauge railway from Siliguri to Darjeeling in West Bengal, run by the Indian Railways. Construction of the railway and machinery of tea production made Nilgiri tea third in the world after China and Ceylon. The "Toy Train" railway carrying passengers, tea and merchandise, was one of the highlights of the Southern Indian trip. But, unfortunately, because of a mudslide a few days before, we did not have a chance to ride on it."

Figure 19 Nilgiri Tea Plantation

C. Mysore Palace

Mysore Palace is one of the "jewel palaces" of southern India, along with the Taj Mahal in the northern part. It was commissioned in 1897 by the Maharani Vani Vilas Sannidhna, the regent of Mysore, and completed in 1912. The palace's architectural style is described commonly as Indo-Saracenic. It blends Hindu, Muslim, Rajput and Gothic architecture. The three storied stone palace, with marble domes and a one thousand four hundred fifteen foot tower (five stories) is surrounded by a large garden. Designed by Henry Irwin, the fine gray granite three storied stone building has deep pink marble domes. There are seven expansive arches on the façade flanking the central arch which is supported by tall pillars, and two more smaller arches included. There is a stunning sculpture of Gajalakshmi, goddess of wealth, prosperity, good luck and abundance with her elephants above the central arch.

The palaces, temples and churches were everywhere. I had to take off my shoes to enter the temples. It was a nuisance, and I really hated it. I wore hiking boots with long laces and several ties. I really hated taking them off and putting them back on again and again. Some temples did not even allow the wearing of socks. Now I understood the reason why the people in India wear sandals, including Mahatma Gandhi. Because of the warm weather, yes, but mostly because they have to remove their shoes so often during the day for worship.

We went with our enthusiastic veteran local guide to the exhibition halls. The beautiful granite reddish gray wall matched the Mysore dynastic families' portraits, which seemed almost alive and ready to speak to us. Invitation boxes from different countries for many occasions were displayed. The metal boxes are silver and gold plated and wooden boxes are beautifully carved. The invitation letters were inside of the boxes. I was amazed by the golden chair for the king and several silver chairs for ministers and the wealth in India for many years; also they were extremely well preserved for centuries. The guide showed us more and more astonishing things, such as the silver-plated or solid silver elevator doors. Every year in September and October the Mysore Dasara festival is held in the courtyard of the palace with several different fields of artists and an old fashioned parade with decorated elephants and carriages which should not be forgotten. The tremendous highlight is more than ninety thousand lights twinkling at night lighting up the palace, but we did not have the opportunity to observe this beautiful scene. The guide told us that Mysore City is the second largest city in the world next to New York City in the consumption of electricity.

D. The Gandhi Museum

The Gandhi Museum is a two-story white building in a small yard, with a black statue of Gandhi standing in the middle of its small yard under the warm afternoon sunlight.

Inside the building are thousands of pictures and photos about India's modern history before Gandhi was born. His family and his pilgrimage through India are exhibited on the walls. When I read and saw the pictures and photos, it was a history lesson on Indian revolution against the British occupation and World War II involvement as Indian soldiers for the British.

In 1915, the Gandhi era began with history books describing Gandhi's "passive resistance", which was adopted by men like Martin Luther King, Jr., trying to demonstrate fighting evil without hating. King did the same non-violence march. Gandhi propagated the boycott of European manufactured clothing, because it made for severe unemployment in India. He personally spun hand-made cloth called Khadi, inexpensive and appropriate for the poor. He taught his countrymen to be self-reliant. Gandhi worked on his spinning wheel (called Charakha) until his death. He felt like he was eating stolen food if he did not work.

I expected more than pictures, photos and posters on the walls, such as the materials he used to use when he was a child and adult life. Nothing was there. Maybe he did not have it.

Finally on August 15, 1947 India gained its independence. The same day, two years earlier, August 15, 1945, Korea became independent from Japan.

Gandhi's blood covered sari from his assassination in January 1948 and his sandals were displayed in the glass cabinets. I expressed great respect for his tireless effort to save his country and people while I was looking at the bloodstained clothes. In my personal opinion, Gandhi's, the father of the modern Indian nation, museum was unbelievably shabby.

Figure 20 Gandhi Museum

Figure 21   At Gandhi's Museum

Figure 22   Gandhi's Museum

E. Kerala

As I mentioned before, the State of Kerala is one of the fifty places to visit in your lifetime recommended by the National Geographic magazine about ten years ago. One year ago they published a new list of fifty places to visit in your lifetime. The State of Kerala is located along the Arabian Sea and Kochi is one of the cities in the Kerala State.

The branches of canals, lagoons and rivers flow into the Arabian Sea. Along the canals, the tall palm trees with coconuts and banana plants welcomed us. A couple of hours of boat riding was so peaceful that it was hard to avoid falling asleep. Occasionally people were doing laundry on the banks of the canals by hitting their clothes on the rocks and cleaning their pans and bowls, too.

Beautiful tourist houseboats passed by with guests. They have a dining area and bedrooms with a western toilet and air conditioning. The cost depends on the accommodations, but we were told that it was about $200 per night per person. They are floating hotels on the canals in the Kerala area. Before the houseboats started as floating hotels on the rivers and canals, they were used as carriers for rice transfers.

Along the bank, under the palm trees, an ice cream shop and shops for fresh coconut juice were unique opportunities we had stepping on the land, which is lower than the canals, like in the Netherlands. A couple of things special in this region are they sow the seeds of rice in the fields, rather than plant each one into the water using the very carefully calculated irrigation systems and harvesting twice per year.

Another unique thing was one man in a small canoe boat was maneuvering about two thousand ducklings and leading them towards the farm. The ducklings all headed in one direction and in one flock. It was like an embroidered black and brown blanket on the water. The canals and rivers are the main transportation method.

Figure 23 House Boat

Figure 24 House Boat

Figure 25   House Boat Town

Figure 26   House Boat Sailing

F. Hindu Temples

Figure 27 Greeting from Holy Elephant

The Hindu temples are all over in India, especially in southern India, few names and just two temples will be described in detail.

Starting with the small temple inside the Mysore Palace, Chamundeshwari Temple in Chamundi Hills, Keshava Temple in Somanathapura, Shore Temple, Five Rathas and cave temples in Mamallapuram, Brihadeshwara Temple in Tanjore, Ucchi Pillayar Temple at Rockfort, Sri Ranganathaswamy Temple in Srirangam and Meenakshi (Sundareshawara) Temple in Madurai.

<u>The Keshava Temple</u> is located in Somnathpur about twenty miles from Mysore City. It was built by the army commander Somnatha under the Hoysala King, Narasimha III. Its unique design and perfect symmetry are similar to Belur and Halebid Temple. It is

in the middle of farm country. Most visitors are foreign tourists rather than local people. The delicate carving on the stone of gods and goddesses and animals, seem as though they were done yesterday, I could even see the delicate fingernails and eyelashes.

The next world famous temple is <u>Meenakshi Sundareswarar (or Amman) Temple</u> in Madurai.

This temple has seven gates in each tower (gopuram). The visitors can go through the first, through third gates, but from the fourth gate only people who worship Hinduism can enter the sanctuary. In Madurai the complex has fourteen towers, including two golden towers. The tallest tower is fifty two meters high. We went into the east tower (gopuram).

In front of the first gate is the main street with the line up of merchandise with souvenirs and small quick bites restaurants. From here we had to take off our shoes. I did not like being on the street with just socks, but luckily they did not ask us to take off our socks too.

Between the gates one, two and three, there are residential areas, apartments with laundry hanging outside the windows. I did not see any white clothes. All of them were gray and dark colors. Downstairs was for the shops and upstairs for residents.

The temple towers on each story have beautiful carvings, all animals, gods and goddesses with different activities. The details and colors of the carvings are awe-inspiring. I cannot write the things on the towers, I can only tell you about the pictures, the art and devotion to religion.

Bani, our guide, told us we had to go to a nearby store and from the top of the store we could see the famous two gold dome towers and would have a closer view of the carvings. That store had much higher quality products than other stores, selling carpets, leather, silk products and souvenirs from brass to stone. I bought a couple of silk scarves and small boxes made from paper.

The rooftop was quite high, maybe four - five stories. We could see clearly the beautiful golden towers and the delicate carvings of the towers. The carvings on the towers are repainted every ten years. The golden dome with its detailed designs is absolutely beautiful. This is one of the greatest remains of Hindu architecture in the world. I was told it is made of pure gold. The dome is protected by electronic sensors and that's why we could not go into the dome area after the fourth gate.

In northern India the Taj Mahal is one of the seven wonders of the world. The Meenakshi Sundareswarar (Amman) Temple in southern India is a precious and beautiful temple, too.

When we were at the third gate at the Meenakshi Sundareswarar Temple I gave an elephant a "nickel". He blessed my head with his trunk for good luck in 2010 and many more years. Whether the elephant is the symbol of god or goddess, I don't know, but the elephant is one of the great tourist attractions in India. This one knew the value of money.

The dancing drama in Kochi "Kathakali" was special and unique. Most of them are male dancers with unique make-up. They showed us the make-up session before the show. They are very famous in Kochi and the people in Kochi are proud of these performances.

Another place we visited was the botanical gardens with special Indian spices and rare plants growing in the private garden which is a well known world wide botanic garden, and is one of eighty in the world. After about an hour tour of this garden we had dinner on banana leaves: chicken curry, vegetable, fish, potato and rice curry. Every dish was with curry.

We followed Indian customs and used our fingers instead of utensils. I forget which hand I used, but it was more difficult to pick up rice curry from banana leaves with my hands than with chopsticks. The dessert was a mixture of rice and sliced banana and watery homemade yoghurt with sugar. While I was licking my fingers, I thought this might be a good business for losing weight in

America, by opening "ten pounds per week losing weight on banana leaves by eating with hands".

In the Kerala region we saw countless attractive houseboats floating under the beautiful sunshine among the palm trees.

* Some of the information in this story was taken from the guidebook provided by the Overseas Adventure Travel (OAT) tour company

Figure 28 Hindu Temples

Figure 29   Details of Sculpture

Figure 30   Hindu Temple

Figure 31 With Hindu Temple Background

Figure 32 India Temple

Cu-Chi Tunnel In Saigon

Christmas time was the perfect time to tour Saigon, Vietnam, to avoid the scorching heat and monsoon season in summer. It was Christmas Eve in 2006 and the waves of bicycles and motorcycles filled the streets in Saigon City. Ladies on bicycles wearing white Vietnamese gowns (kind of uniform) with cone shaped straw hats in the midst of traffic were the most beautiful scenes I saw.

I thought Vietnam was a Buddhist country, but Saigon was already contaminated by the commercial promotion of Christmas. Christmas trees were at the corner of the street decorated with unique ornaments with small or large crosses. Christmas decorations on the windows and inside the stores were not different from our usual advertisements. The small blinking lights, big Santa with "Ho Ho" smile and reindeer pulling the sled with stacks of boxes, but no signs of celebrations of the Buddhist events were observed.

In the middle of the 1950s, we had an almost identical experience in Korea, like Vietnam today. We took advantage of the Christmas spirit to avoid the curfew, which prohibited the people from being on the street after midnight. The only exceptions were Christmas and New Year's Eve. There was no curfew for these two nights. Non-Christians enjoyed this occasion more than Christians because of the freedom to drink and stroll on the streets all night long, especially young people who were dating.

We came out from downtown Saigon, which was in a joyful Christmas mood, and went into a tropical forest, which is twenty miles away from the city in order to visit the "Cu-Chi Tunnel". Our guide was my height, five feet four inches, and weighed less than one hundred lbs. He was very thin, like a toothpick, but as strong as steel nails, with a dark brown complexion.

"We will walk about a mile to the forest from the place we park our bus." He warned us in a husky voice that we had to walk inside the forest. "Cu-Chi tunnel is in the forest, about one mile away from the sea shore". The plants in the forest were knee high and small trees with dried leaves covered the area. Was this the result of brush fires or heavy bombing in this area by the American Army to smoke out the Viet Cong? The forest was not dense like a tropical one. "The trees are quite small, like just planted," I asked our guide and continued, "On the TV news usually the Viet Cong came out with their hands up to their ears from the dense tropical areas with tall trees which had huge leaves," and I continued, "Inside the tropical area was the perfect place for the Viet Cong to hide. But this area strangely does not have many trees." I looked at his face expecting correct answers. "You will find out the reason later." That was his quick answer.

The houses, which had only thatch straw roofs without any walls on stilts, were seen along the seashore which used to be the communication center of the Viet Cong at night and, during the daytime, it was as an ordinary household. Dried brown leaves were scattered on the ground. It indicated that it was autumn in the end of December in Vietnam.

"Around here is the entrance to the tunnel. Please, find the hole or entrance to the tunnel." The guide showed about fifteen - twenty yards of the radius of the locations and continued, "In fifteen minutes, please. Now it is easier to find it than in the summer, because the plants are shorter and less dense." Then he was quiet and gave us only fifteen minutes to find the tunnel entrance. Everybody was anxious to find a hole (or holes) in the ground. Time was ticking. After ten minutes nobody had any luck. Bob from Illinois was desperate and asked the guide after several sweeps of leaves around with his feet, "Is the hole big or small? What is the size, approximately?" The guide gave him an unfavorable answer with a grin on his face, "I cannot tell you. Please try, you will find it."

"Kwang, there are no footprints, no clues at all," I spoke to him with astonishment at their clever hiding skills. "No. We could not." Kwang picked up a stick one inch diameter, four feet high and was tapping around on the ground in order to find any weak spots which would lead to the hole.

Our group was spread around inside the radius, twenty yards. "We all give up," we all screamed at once to our guide. He came to us from five yards away with an ugly smile on his face. "Look here. Is there any difference in the ground?" Then he pointed out the place under our feet covered with dry brown, yellow and green leaves. "No. Absolutely no difference," Victoria commented, and our guide did not miss his triumphant moment, "No, you cannot." Then he pushed away the leaves and under the leaves was about one inch of thick soil covering a thick steel plate over a tiny hole. The hole size was about eighteen inches by sixteen inches, could be less than that. The steel plate size was twenty inches by eighteen inches by one inch thickness. I could not believe such a small entrance led to the tunnel.

Our surprise left us speechless. Everybody was quiet and looked at the small hole. Kwang and I thought *People could absolutely not go in and out of this hole, unless they were rats*.

"You can come down with me and look inside the tunnel." After this he hesitated for a moment and tried to choose the right words indicating that coming down to the tunnel was not for everybody, because of weight or claustrophobia. He did not use the word "overweight", and mentioned that, "If you have any fear of confined spaces, I really do not recommend it," he concluded his recommendation. According to his standards all of us were overweight, except me.

Everybody was looking at each other – who should be the next in line after the guide? Then the attention focused on me because our group thought I was the smallest after the guide. Without any special reason actually, I was scared to death, and thought what if I go down and never come back again. I looked at Kwang. Kwang understood my feelings. Without a single word, by reading my face, he started to descend after the guide and I followed him.

"It is just like a spider web," I exclaimed. "And, actually it is." My tremendous fear of tiny spaces was gone when I took my first step on the ladder by putting my left hand on my left ear in order to save space between my shoulder and the wall, and my right one holding the rungs of the ladder.

"Wow. I did not stick to the entrance. I made it," I screamed with excitement, but I could not avoid touching my shoulders on the walls.

One half of our group started to descend into the tunnel. A small steel ladder was almost straight up to the wall. After four or five steps down, he led us to the first floor to the bigger round space for the officer's room, kitchen and dining room. Then one more story down again, a huge open area for a meeting place and small tunnel spaces connected each other, similar to a spider web. All the rooms were wide and spacious. A couple of stories down from the second floor was another entrance leading to the third and fourth stories down. The entrance was much smaller than the entrance from the ground. People, particularly the enemy could be trapped there without any resistance. "What a shrewd design," I whispered to Kwang, "This entrance is the second barrier of defense without using any weapons."

Small wells or cisterns were wisely installed inside the tunnel but they seemed all dried. In order to disguise the smoke from cooking, the smoke was dispersed through the tunnels inside so that no smoke came out at all from one single tunnel. The floor was an uneven dirt floor and electrical wires were dangling over the ceiling. Some walls, damaged by air bombing, barely stood with support from steel beams. We only stayed at the second floor from the ground and observed the structure of the tunnel. Everyone had different thoughts about the Viet Cong's activities inside the tunnel. Unfortunately, we could not go down further to the third and fourth floor because the structure was not sturdy enough to hold all the people. When we came out, we screamed with great relief and joy. "What an experience, we are glad we came out from such a tiny hole."

Half of our group who could not go into the tunnel felt jealous and curious, but were happy to see that we all came out without incident. Bob asked me, "You will go down again?" "Once is enough." That was my simple and firm answer.

Nobody knew there were tunnels at this particular location until the Vietnam War was over. So, in the daytime, nobody was seen in the jungle, but after dark the U.S. Army got attacked by the Viet Cong from nowhere in an avalanche, like ghosts. Also, the most amazing thing was the tunnels were near villages and the seashore in order to get supplies easily. The U.S. army never could find the tunnel locations, even though they were aware that the tunnels existed.

While we were walking towards the bus, Bob and Victoria, who could not enter the tunnel, were vigorously discussing our big mistake was involvement in the Vietnam War.

Surprisingly they almost yelled at each other about the differences of interpretation of the Vietnam War, especially about the tunnel structure and its functions. Bob had great interest in and had studied about the tunnels before he came on this trip. I heard the words over my shoulder from them "black echo", "carpet bombing", "crimp of the opening" and "tunnel rats". The reason for the yelling match between Bob and Victoria was whether or not the American Army found the tunnels. Victoria said "no" … Bob said "yes".

The truth was a specialist enemy troop from Australia under the command of Captain Sandy MacGregor did venture into the tunnels where they found ammunition, radio equipment, medical supplies and food, as well as signs of considerable Viet Cong presence. Following the troops' discovery in Cu Chi, Sandy MacGregor was awarded the Military Cross.

Later I found out what the words Bob and Victoria had been using meant, some of them were new to me. "Black echo" described the terrible condition of the Viet Cong's tunnel life among the unbearable attack of ants, poisonous centipedes, scorpions, spiders and vermin. The greatest concern was lack of supplies, but our guide never mentioned this extremely difficult condition.

"Carpet bombing" as the words indicate, bombing by B-52 in the Cu Chi area, like a spreading carpet.

"Tunnel rats", after the Australian troops' successful discovery of the Cu Chi tunnels, Sandy MacGregor referred to his men as tunnel ferrets at an international press conference in Saigon. An American journalist, having never heard of ferrets, used the term tunnel rats and it stuck.

The Cu-Chi Tunnel was an unforgettable historical event, but now, believe it or not, it is a tourist spot. The brilliant strategy for winning the war against a huge country like America that has abundant human and natural resources, especially newly developed weapons was amazing. While Kwang and I were following the group and guide to the bus, both of us were speechless and thinking, "What a terrible war that was."

Figure 33 Inside Cu Chi Tunnel

Figure 34 Conference Room in Cu Chi Tunnel

Figure 35 Cu Chi Tunnel Entranc

Dandong

Dandong is the border city between North Korea and China, actually Manchuria, divided by the Yalu River which has its origin from Lake Chonji (means Heaven Lake) and is the longest river in North Korea.

About one thousand years ago, Dandong belonged in the territory of Korya, one of the dynasties in Korean history. The Yalu River is the bloodstream of North Korea. It produces electricity, transportation channel, fishing industry and attracts year round tourism.

In April, our yearly visit at Shenyang Lusan Technology in Shenyang, China for our annual Board of Director's meeting lasted for three - four days and we returned to Korea without any sightseeing. This year our employees took us to Dandong to tour historical places from the Korean War.

Rain drops were getting bigger and bigger when we arrived in Dandong after a five hour drive from Shenyang. The rain in April in Northern China was chilly. Under the rain we strolled across the old bridge on the Yalu River which was built by the Japanese in 1930 and was destroyed by American attacks during the Korean War in the 1950's. China built a new bridge between North Korea and China but they left the old bridge as a memorial of the bloody Korean War. I stood at the edge of the bridge which was the last piece of cement hanging on the water and looked over at North Korea with the very dim hope that I could find my birthplace at Baekdu Mountain.

The only thing spreading in front of my eyes on the North Korean side was the black soil without any crops. Maybe it was too early to put the seeds under the ground, especially because of the cold front from Manchuria. I could not see any high rise buildings, even one-story buildings, like in Dandong where there are many higher than ten story office buildings and apartments. Far, far away a couple of chimneys jumped out from nowhere. There was no smoke or steam from the chimneys

Before checking into the hotel, after lunch, we started a tour around the Yalu River. We had about a forty five minute boat ride along the Yalu River on the Chinese side. Our boat would cruise almost in the middle of the Yalu River but sometimes intentionally or not the boat was close to the North Korean side. Several rusty boats were docking on the shore and a couple of people in green uniforms were doing repair work on the boat on the North Korean side. We waved our hands but they just looked at us, showing no interest and no curiosity. In contrast, the shining colorful tourist boats were waiting for the guests on the Dandong side and, along the riverbank, the beautiful park was developed with monuments and a series of restaurants, especially Korean restaurants. Alas, on the North Korean side, there was nothing.

The Hotel Pacifica in Dandong was generally clean and our room was clean and roomy with a teapot and TV set which was broadcasting the Korean programs from South Korea. The lobby was busy and noisy with a group of people for parties. The cars on the streets were a variety of brands from all over the world: Benz, Ford, Lexus, Volkswagen and Cadillac.

Luckily, by the next morning the rain stopped. The hotel was located a couple of blocks away from the Yalu River and the park. Kwang went by foot to the park and observed the activities. Groups of people exercised in the park: Tai Chi, yoga, running along the track, ballroom dancing with loud music from the jukebox and voice exercises with high-pitched notes.

When we came back from the park, the red plastic balloon arch stood in front of the entrance to the hotel. The size of the arch was ten feet tall, eight feet wide and about one and one-half feet diameter. The red arch indicated wedding ceremonies and receptions. The bride entered this arch with the Chinese traditional cart carried by four men and, after passing through the arch, the bride got off the cart and entered the hotel. Then she changed her clothes to the white western style wedding gown.

After breakfast we went to the top of Tiger Mountain, where the Great Wall started. The length was about a one hour walk up to the top and one half hour down. It was a very easy and comfortable course for hiking and with constant repairs and maintenance all the stones were in the right places. In the watchtowers there were holes for guns or bow and arrow shooting. I deeply admired their technology. At the top we could see the wide black fields in North Korea.

The final stop was the Korean Memorial Tower which was built in July 1993, forty years after the Korean War ended, and the Korean War museum. On display outside of the museum were Russian made tanks, airplanes, equipment and trucks. Inside the museum there are many pictures and scenes of battlegrounds, refugees, soldiers and generals' pictures on the walls. It is quite a collection. In one glass cabinet there was the famous letter from Kim, Il Sung and Park, Hyunyang to Mao Tse Tung asking his assistance during the Korean War in neat Korean characters signed by both in Chinese characters.

In the late afternoon we came to the border area between the two nations on the land, China and North Korea. A small stream was running between them and I could put my feet on the North Korean side with an easy jump.

I looked around. No guards from North Korea were seen. Nobody was there.

"Temptation. Temptation".

I wanted to jump to the North Korean side and come back quickly. I could not. My fear would not allow it. Mrs. Liu, Nancy and I had a Kodak moment at the border holding the monument stone which was engraved, "One step jump" which meant one step jump to North Korea.

I want to make two things very clear to my readers, especially those that do not have experience or knowledge of the Korean War, that the Korean War was not started by South Korea as indicated in the Korean War Museum in Dandong and other places. At that moment South Korea was not ready to invade the other country. (This is only my personal opinion). The second, most important thing is that Manchuria was our land and in our territory during the Koryo dynasty about one thousand years ago. During the Koryo dynasty Manchuria was an area larger than South and North Korea combined.

Figure 36 One Step Jump to North Korea

Figure 37 Yalu River Bridge

Figure 38 Memorial Tower

The Pyongyang House, Shenyang, China

Every year in April, Kwang and I visit the Shenyang Lusan Lubrication Technology Co., Ltd. in Shenyang, China, which is about two hundred miles northeast of Beijing. Shenyang, in old Manchuria, is the fourth largest city in China and it has built a solid reputation for a heavy defense industry, such as cannon manufacturing. It also hosted soccer games at the 2008 Summer Olympics at the new stadium. Shenyang Lusan Lubrication Technology Co., Ltd. is a joint venture company with Chrysan Industries, Inc., Plymouth, Michigan, USA.

During our three to four day stay in Shenyang we spent most of our time having plant tours at customer locations and business meetings without any sight seeing in the city and its vicinity. The best highlight of the events was the evening activities: tasting extremely authentic Chinese food at a variety of specialty restaurants. You would be so enthralled by the taste that you wouldn't notice if the people at the other end of the table died.

One typical example is the specialty restaurant for fish. The live fish were swimming in large water tanks which have more than two hundred gallon capacity with constant circulation of water with bubbling air. The fish tanks are near the reception desk where guests can see the fish when entering the restaurant. I could see not only fish, but also small octopus, abalones, crabs and New Zealand lobsters in the tanks. We picked the live trout from the tank and asked the waitress to have it steamed and served with sweet and sour sauce with green onions on the top. Another example was the vegetable dishes. On one occasion there were twenty two different vegetable dishes for only twelve people. The portions were small but it was very impressive to offer such a variety of vegetable dishes prepared by different cooking methods. Cold, steamed, sautéed, fried with different seasonings, with cucumbers, eggplant, cabbage, bok choy, green onions, peas, carrots, broccoli, seaweed, squash and peanuts with beef.

Over the last ten years during our visits to Shenyang we went to a Korean restaurant a couple of times. Our Korean origins led our staff to think that we might miss the Korean food after only a couple of days in China. The Korean population in Shenyang is very large. They are the descendants of immigrants to Shenyang before and during World War II. They were farmers who wanted to have their own land in the new world in Manchuria which has endless territory with rich soil. The other groups were organized patriots who fought for Korean independence against the Japanese occupation in Manchuria after escaping from Korea in the 1930s. Now they operate restaurants and are owners of small businesses in the city. On the street we can read the Korean letters on the boards "Chosun Bulgogi" (Korean barbecue) and others in a combination of Chinese and Korean letters. I was told that the Korean community is the largest ethnic minority in Shenyang. In China and Japan they call Koreans "Chosun".

When I first walked on the street in Shenyang in 1994, donkeys were pulling carts and a wave of bicycles was covering the street and very few cars were seen. Furthermore, there were no big trucks. Actually tractors were hauling the heavy farm produce in a trailer. The buildings were gray or almost black from the smoke and dust. Run down buildings were everywhere, with laundry hanging from the windows. For decades under communist control nobody cared about the public property or even their own apartment because the apartment was owned by the communist government. I did not see anyone wearing white clothes. Rather, they had turned gray or dark gray from the original white. The dentist on the street, holding a pair of pliers in his hand, had one stool and wore a gray coat which was supposed to be white.

Now Shenyang has torn down almost all of the old buildings and erected high-rise office buildings, new hotels and has even created an apartment district. Waves of cars replaced bicycles on the streets. A four or six lane highway on each side is not enough to prevent traffic jams during rush hours. Shenyang has become one of the largest and most modern cities in China and maybe in Asia and Europe, compared to the two-lane highway with donkeys, bicycles and people of fifteen years ago. The streets and highways seem to be an exhibition place for Cadillac, Benz, Buick, Hyundai, Toyota, Volkswagen, representing worldwide car manufacturers. World famous brands of cosmetics, handbags, clothes, are sold at much higher prices in the department stores than at their origin. In China about one percent of their population of three billion people are millionaires and have huge buying power.

On April first every year the city of Shenyang cuts the heating system, maybe all over China. April in Shenyang without any heat inside the buildings is fairly cold. Even if I wore a heavy sweater, my hands and feet were frozen during the meeting. To get warmer I had soup for lunch and continuously drank hot tea, warming my hands on the teacups.

While holding warm teacups in both hands, I thought about the soups for dinner, seafood soup, chicken noodle or vegetable soup, which I had at several different restaurants. Through my imagination even the smell of steaming soup touched my nose and spread through my body to raise my body temperature a couple of degrees.

Our General Motors van parked in front of the "Pyongyang House". *Oh, no, another Korean restaurant.* I murmured to myself with disappointment. *If I am in China I would rather have rare authentic Chinese food.* Contrary to my choice, our staff chose a Korean restaurant to make our stay more comfortable and enjoyable in China. It would have been a more memorable experience if I had authentic Chinese food. In 1994 I tasted a snake dish with typical Chinese gravy sauce on the top. If they did not mention it was snake there was absolutely no way I could guess it was snake. I thought it was a portion of chicken neck with soft bones.

I was told that an extremely rare delicacy is a dish with mosquito eyes which is only for Chinese emperors. It will be a great honor and pleasure if I could see the dish with mosquito eyes and much better if I would be able to taste it.

Several steps in front of the building two busboys led us to the door and two ladies in very simple Korean dress opened the door and spoke in Chinese "Welcome? or good evening?" with a ninety degree bow. I smiled back at them. "xiexie" (In Chinese Thank you.). I am using "xiexie" with a smile everywhere, every time, even if it does not fit the occasion well. Fish smells, but an indescribable unique Chinese seasoning smell opened my sensory tissues instead of Korean kimchee with spicy and strong garlic smell.

Two white porcelain vases, about five feet tall, stood near the stairs without any plants in them, but the pictures on the vases were beautiful with azalea flowers, pine trees in the mountains, small streams running among rocks and a couple of Chinese angels floated among the flowers on the wall of the vases. I followed the hostess wearing a light pink Korean dress through a dark corridor and several steps to the second floor which was made of black granite. She led us to a private room with a karaoke setting. Instead of room numbers, each room had flower names: azalea, chrysanthemum or magnolia.

There are more than twenty private rooms on the second floor with six to twenty people capacities. The loud noise was unavoidable from the other rooms, even with the doors closed. We went into an "azalea" room for ten people with two young waitresses who were tall, with healthy, beautiful faces, wearing simple traditional Korean dresses waiting for us.

In South Korea the traditional women's dresses are beautiful with colorful long skirts designed with a golden seal and the tops matched the colors and designs for the skirt. Sometimes the fabric of the sleeves is rainbow pattern. The fabric is silk in winter for warmth and threads of Mariana in summer to avoid the heat and the sticky humidity. These materials were used for making ropes and fishing nets years ago.

Casual greetings were exchanged between the waitresses and our staff in Chinese. The big surprise was their happy and healthy appearance. I had heard that people in North Korea were impoverished and starving, but these waitresses looked very healthy, with no sign of malnutrition. They handed over a thick menu with pictures of dishes written in both Korean and Chinese. The picture of a small palace was on the front cover of the menu. A couple of dishes were recommended by Kwang and we asked our staff for their choices. Of course, they did not forget to include Chinese beer "Thin Tau".

Since the waitresses were informed that we were Korean we started speaking Korean. At first their heavy accents from Pyongyang Province in North Korea scratched my eardrums uncomfortably, but we had no problems understanding each other. With curiosity I started, "Have you been here for a long time? Your Chinese is impeccable." "About two years ago we came for a training program in business operations." One of the tall ladies answered my unexpected questions while the other lady was busy getting the order from our staff. "Is this restaurant owned by the North Korean government or privately owned?" my explosion of curiosity continued. Kwang pinched me to signal no more questions. The tall lady asked politely, avoiding my question, "Father, (respectful expression, instead of Mr. so and so) How long will you stay in Shenyang?" Kwang's answers were quick and short in an effort to escape more questions from them. Then the food was on the table ... spicy kimchee, bulgogi, bindaeduck (Korean pancake with vegetables and pork), vegetable dishes and small, grilled flounder with head and tail of one fish for one person. The flounder was dried first and then grilled. The servings were simple, and the presentations were not adequate, without decorations like Japanese dishes, but they were clean. The serving dishes were marked as "Pyongyang House" in Chinese.

Under the South Korean Presidents, Kim Dae-jung and Rho Moo Hyun, the South Korean government sent unbelievable amounts of aid to North Korea; rice, cows and even created the Kaisung Industrial Park in the North Korean side in order to utilize excess North Korean labor to produce products and export them worldwide.

From these activities the South Korean government did not get any significant return from North Korea. It was only a one-way street. The President Kim Dae-jung was the first president from South Korea to visit North Korea and he met Kim Jong Il in Pyongyang for discussions about the unification of both Koreas, but President Kim was too naïve to understand Kim Jong Il's duplicity. President Kim Dae-jung received the Nobel Peace Prize in 2000 for his fruitless efforts at unification. All these events flashed through my mind like a movie screen.

"Mother, this droomm (vegetable like asparagus but with a softer texture) came directly from Pyongyang especially for this restaurant." I know droomm which is a wild vegetable growing on deep mountains like ginseng and is only available in early spring. It is rare and a delicacy. "Thank you. I know droomm. It comes from a deep mountain at high altitude." "Mother, how do you know droomm?" the smaller lady asked me in surprise. Her eyelids almost touched her eyebrows. "I was born in North Korea near Mt. Baekdu."

We were busy having dinner and everybody was so quiet enjoying their meals. The tall lady asked me, "Mother, I heard you are from America. How is the life in America?" She did not have time to stop, "Are your brothers and sisters still in South Korea? She persisted, "You must miss them deeply, and you would definitely have a much better life in your native country." I was in a serious intelligence war between the North Korean waitresses and myself. All my hairs were standing straight up from tension. I was struggling, how could I answer her questions? I needed time to give her some answers, and now the most important thing for me was to get information about life in North Korea. This was a most difficult task. Maybe it is easier to land on the moon than to collect information on North Korea from these two ladies. Instead of an immediate and direct answer I asked her, "How does your government select students to send abroad for business training?" The direction of our conversation was twisted. While I was waiting for her answer I earned the time for her previous questions. "Of course, it is best living in your native country with your relatives and friends, but we have been in America for over forty years. America is my country and I feel a native."

Our intelligence war reached its peak, "How is the job stability?" the short lady asked me, pretending she had not listened to my previous comments, and expecting my answer to be, "The job market is very gloomy. No hope at all under the present recession, especially for immigrants." Instead I spoke quietly with a grin on my face. "It is fairly comfortable. Everywhere is the same wherever you are. Sometimes it is difficult and sometimes it is easier." They were disappointed again by my vague, unfocused comments.

Kwang pinched me again. I had to stop the conversation. I decided to enjoy my food but I was not thrilled with the taste of it. In Korea each province has a slightly different style of food. The Pyongyang House is adapted to serve Chinese and Korean residents in China. The menus are adjusted to meet local demand.

I was very cold at the meeting and having a seesaw game of intelligence with North Koreans in the restaurant it seemed that I was chewing sand in my mouth instead of the delicious Pyonyang food.

While we were enjoying dinner with lively conversation among our employees, the tall lady had disappeared and only the smaller lady kept serving us with tea and Chinese wine. Our staff was in a good mood with the spicy food and bulgogi. I could not control my curiosity or my eagerness to get information on life in North Korea. "Are there many restaurants like this in China?" "They are in almost every city, mother." It was a short and very blunt answer from the smaller lady indicating that my question was nonsense, and the message was very strong, "Please, no more questions."

Kwang pinched me again violently. I was at the brink of screaming.

After dinner we came out to the large hall which has about fifty tables and in front of the tables an entertainment stage was set up. We saw the tall lady who had been serving us playing drums with five band members in a joyful mood and a lady was singing a song in Chinese in front of the tables. All the guests were enjoying the band and the songs while they were having dinner. The hall was full. I did not see any empty tables.

The North Korean government sent students for training in business practice. They are multi-talented students from higher ranking families within the communist party.

In the van, Mr. Li (the general manager from Shenyang Lusan, our company) talked with Kwang about the dinner through the interpreter. I could not describe my feelings. I just remember that I tried to dig about the North Korean economy and living standards through the two ladies and the ladies tried to please us by calling us "father and mother" without telling any stories about life in North Korea.

The driver opened the window of the van. The chilly air woke me from my fantasy and disarray. *How stupid I was to try to find out about their life in North Korea from these royal communist party students.* Then I remembered when I was in Dandong, the border city between China and North Korea divided by the Yalu River, the placard on the North Korean side says "Kim Jong Il is the sun in the twenty first century." The people in North Korea are worshipping Kim Jong Il as a god. With my ignorance and lack of knowledge of Korean politics, I well deserved getting pinched by Kwang ... but *Can I visit my birthplace in North Korea during my lifetime?*

Even if my bruise on my thigh disappeared in a couple of months, the puzzle in my mind "Can I visit my birthplace in North Korea in my lifetime?" was not solved.

Figure 39 PyungYang House

Ger Tent Camp in Mongolia

In August 2011, I had a great deal of curiosity, equal anxiety, and concerns on the accommodations and meals for a three week nomadic Mongolian trip. On several other trips, the travel agents sent us a detailed description of the itinerary and the hotel information before our departure for our trip. This time I just went there without any information on the levels of hardness of traveling and accommodations. *If you are looking for comfort like your own bed and home, then you'd better stay home.* This is my philosophy all the time before I leave my house to travel, so I was happy wherever, whenever I went. I did not have many complaints. But this time without any guidelines, I was told by Kwang, "We will stay in a tent." "Okay in a tent for twenty days." I talked back to him without looking at his face and continued, "It's no big deal. We did it in Africa and Patagonia. No problem. We can handle it." I showed him a positive attitude. "Good. We can make it." He was relieved.

Mongolia is not a nation in the TV news spotlight like Libya or Greece in recent political and economic turmoil. Very seldom does it appear in the news.

My knowledge is very limited relating to Mongolia, it is mostly about Genghis Khan, the Gobi Desert and the origin of Koreans and American Indians is Mongolia. So, Koreans have the unique "Mongolian blue spot" (birthmark) on their buttocks.

The tent meant "Ger" by Kwang's definition where Mongolian nomadic people live. We stayed sixteen days in Ger camps, two days in a pop tent in the yard of the nomadic family in Ger, and luckily, two days in a bed and breakfast hotel in Ulaanbaatar, the capital city of Mongolia. The total population of Mongolia is only two million seven hundred thousand with 1.5

million square kilometers of a vast land, and about seven hundred thousand people living in Ulaanbaatar.

When we arrived at Genghis Khan Airport on August 14, 2011 it was mid-morning. It was a very small airport with only one conveyor belt for baggage pick-ups. We took a taxi from the airport to the Voyage Plus hotel, which is just a bed and breakfast with very simple accommodations. The two-way highway was paved, but many potholes and the bumpy road with gravel gave us a Mongolian massage.

Along the road one or two story houses were inside five - six feet high wooden fences. Occasionally I could see the white "Ger" among the buildings. The Ger is a nomadic tent, which is moved around from place to place on the prairie with herds of cattle, horses, goats, sheep and yaks. After dismantling, it can be rebuilt, easily and fast.

Our main guide was Pascal from France, who is the lead guide for the nomadic Mongolian trips from the Canadian company, G.A.P., Great Adventure People.

The local Mongolian guide, Suke, three drivers and ten tourists left the hotel with several four-wheel drive Land Cruisers. The travelers were two American (us), four Canadians, two U.K., one Australian and one Italian with age ranges from twenty one to seventy seven years old. Of course, we were the two oldest people but were the most active people except for the two guides.

In eighteen days, we traveled from Ulaanbaatar to Horbund, Gobi Desert near the border of China, through Great White Lake, Lake Khovsgal near the Russian border and came back to Ulaanbaatar. We visited almost every important place in Mongolia, which covered one fifth of the total area of the country.

Our Number One car driver was Tomoroo, Number Two Tseemee, and Number Three Namhai, who was heavy and liked to drink vodka, and all the time he felt hot, and did not wear any shirt, even if we wore warm jackets. His round belly was always showing without any cover. Our Number Two driver, Tseemee, was in

Korea for three years, working in the jeans and plastic container manufacturing plants, because of much higher wages than in Mongolia and opportunities for learning advanced manufacturing methods and management skills in Korea. Later I found out that many Mongolians are in South Korea working at the plants, in the fields and as domestic helpers.

After twenty minutes driving, we came to the outskirts of Ulaanbaatar and started driving on the dusty, bumpy road through the vast prairie of semi-desert. Actually there was no road, per se; the drivers drove by creating road towards the direction we were heading. Very tiny, short brown grass, maybe four – five inches high, was on the ground. The cars were driving in the midst of white clouds of dust. Without seeing the cars in front of us, we could only see white clouds moving. Whenever the four-wheel Land Cruiser crossed the creeks and quite deep small rivers, and climbed the hilly mountain, I held Kwang's hand tightly, even though our drivers had unbelievable driving skills.

The herds of goats, sheep and cows were lying down peacefully on the prairie and enjoying the warm autumn sunbeams. For a distance, the white Gers were scattered on the wide open land like white cotton balls. Of course, we stopped to take unique pictures for Kodak moments. The white, brown and white and black spotted sheep were flocked together like huge rocks in the land. It was absolutely amazing scenery and one cannot have such an experience in any other place in the world. Another most stunning view was the bald mountain without any grass or trees that stood at the end of the prairie.

Before we arrived at the first Ger camp we stopped for a box lunch on the hillside off the road in the middle of the vast land of Mongolia, looking down on the herds of brown cows, horses and black yaks. A nice breeze helped us escape from the direct sunlight shining on our faces.

During our day long driving we seldom saw cars, just two or three times we saw Russian made vans with tourists. The reason was that late August is the end of the tourist season, and the world economy prohibited luring more tourists to remote Mongolia.

The Gers are five to ten miles apart where the flocks of herds were wandering on the brown field. They were controlled by shepherds on the horses or on motorcycles. Usually the Gers stood as a single unit, even if they were together, the distance between two Gers was at least two hundred – three hundred yards apart.

Horbund was the first Ger camp, where we stayed overnight and then moved on to the different locations with the almost identical structure Ger camp. Two or three people could be accommodated inside the Ger. From tonight I would have a unique nomadic life experience staying in a Ger. I sentenced myself to a very uncomfortable journey staying in a Ger, not even in a bed and breakfast hotel. One of my friends made a comment that whenever we travel, we go to places that demand extra physical activities, "Kook-Wha you are spending big bucks to take uncomfortable and harsh journeys. I absolutely do not understand it." His voice making this comment was ringing in my ears.

Inside three simple single beds were located around the wall. To my surprise, instead of sleeping on the ground with a sleeping bag, I will sleep in a bed. I was so happy. "Wow. A bed. It is nice and the sheets are clean," I screamed and continued, "Kwang, you fooled me. You told me we were going to sleep on the ground and in a sleeping bag."

"I thought that, too," he told me very quietly.

We put our daypacks and cameras down on one of the extra beds and looked around the inside. The round open window without glass on the top was half open and half covered with felt. In the middle of the Ger a pole supports the main structure of the Ger and a huge rock (one foot by one and one-half feet), weighing maybe twenty pounds, was dangling. *Why is a rock in the middle of Ger?* I mentioned to myself and asked Kwang.

"Mmm, I do not know. It is strange." At that moment Pascal came to check that everybody was satisfied with Ger's condition.

"Fine. Fine. Pascal, by the way, why is the heavy rock dangling in the middle of Ger?" We both questioned at the same time. With his French accent, Pascal gave us the unbelievable answer, "That's odd, isn't it, but the purpose of the rock in the middle is to prevent Ger from blowing away by strong wind." We all laughed. Then he left us to check on other people.

"Should be another method to prevent blowing away of Ger in strong winds," Kwang commented as an engineer. While we are waiting to bring our luggage from the car, we looked carefully inside again. The bed sheets were very clean and the pillows were filled with buckwheat, it was heavy, and the pillow cover was a small hand towel. At the bottom a Ger has many small holes, where cats or rats or any animals can come in and out. Also, the cool wind could blow in the warm air through the bottom holes. The floor was not dirt. On the cement foundation they put a small thin area rug and vinyl sheet with a wooden floor pattern. Later I was told by Pascal about the structure of Ger: the main parts of Ger are: toono, uni, bagano, wall and felt.

Toono is the top part of a Ger and its shape is like a round wooden wheel, which is the function of the window that the light can penetrate. It does not have glass. When we arrived at the camp it was half closed, but if we wanted to close it, there is a string attached to the toono from outside. Uni is the support structure made of a round roof with straight long wooden sticks seven to ten feet long, depending on the size. Bagana is the columns, and the most important elements of it. Two baganas are the main structural support and it has beautiful paintings on the surface. The walls are cross-knitted with thin wood two inches wide by one-half inch thick around the round wall like wigwag type and felt covers the wall all around. The door of the Ger mainly consists of a frame and boards only about four feet high. The right and left edges of the walls are connected to the left and right side of the doorframe. Several times Kwang and I hit the top of the door without thinking that the height of the door is only four feet. The most amazing thing is the Ger does not have any nails to connect the structures and the knots are made of yaks thread.

The public facility and shower rooms were tolerable. They built these Ger camps on the prairie for a hotel, but they were not maintained well, and we barely managed with warm water for a shower.

Pascal came again. "Dinner is 7:00 p.m. and we will have electricity between 8:30 and 10:00 p.m. Charge the camera battery during this period."

Around the camp the weeds grew to the knees. Sometimes the cows came to the camp grazing the weeds. At 7:00 p.m. we went to the dining Ger which was bigger than ours and was nicely decorated, even a sofa at the entrance near the door and a couple of travel magazines on the small table. In one corner was a small bar dais where wine glasses were dangling from the ceiling and there was Genghis Khan Beer in bottles in the cooler.

Big pictures of Genghis Khan were on the walls, when he was young and old. In Mongolia almost everything is connected to Genghis Khan: Genghis Khan Bank, Genghis Khan Beer, Genghis Khan Restaurant, Genghis Khan Airport, and Genghis Khan Museum. I cannot list all the names.

The dining room in the Ger was clean and warm. The first course was shredded cabbage with mayonnaise, and the main dish was yak stew, steamed rice and steamed mixed vegetables. The short grain steamed rice and yak stew were delicious. The dessert was a small chocolate bar. In Mongolia most of the people's main meal is meat. For breakfast, lunch, dinner, everyone has to eat meat. I enjoyed the dinner exceptionally because of the yak beef stew and steamed rice and coffee with a chocolate bar. I did not see any fat people in Mongolia, even with a meat diet, they surely look very slim.

After dinner around 8:30 p.m. it was still daylight, twilight hadn't come yet. We strolled a while around the campgrounds. Actually, this camp is located in the vast prairie, with no other camps around. We are just between sky and land.

We came into our Ger and put the flashlight under the heavy buckwheat pillow. I tried to fall asleep without thinking about having to go to the facility in the middle of the night without Kwang. Visiting the facility was the biggest problem I had at night.

But we had an unexpected concern. Near midnight Kwang and I woke up because of the cold. It was freezing. We tossed around on the squeaky bed trying to get warm. "Kwang, the bed may be broken. I am tossing around too much," and continued, "It is getting really cold."
"Yes, it is desert weather. I forgot. The daytime is hot and the night is cold."
"Let's take out our sleeping bag," was my suggestion.
"Maybe, or we can wear more layers of clothing instead of taking out the sleeping bag. It is at the bottom of our luggage," was Kwang's suggestion.

Without any comment about Kwang's suggestion, we both started to put on our pants and sweaters over our pajamas and socks too. We tried to sleep. After a few minutes Kwang started to snore. He was tired? Or the extra clothes made him warm enough? He fell asleep. I could not sleep and I was still very cold. I made a squeaky noise from the bed and pulled out a blanket from the extra bed and put it on my bed and covered my eyes with my hands. I hope it is getting warmer.

Figure 40   In front of Ger Tent

85

Figure 41 Ger Camp

Figure 42 Mogolia's Most Dangerous Bridge

Family Dinner in Mongolia

Today will be the first family dinner after several days with unique, unusual experiences at the Ger camps. After staying overnight in the Ger camps, it becomes as routine as hopping from hotel to hotel. All of us were excited about a family dinner at a home, not in Ger, the expectation being another new adventure in Mongolia. I thought that at least it should be different from the simple and primitive Ger camp.

Bumpy roads, crossing creeks, climbing the hills with the Land Cruiser, dust penetrated through the windows, and the loud Mongolian music from the CD filled the car. It was like Russian military marching music. It prohibited falling asleep in the car. It was like marching to the Promised Land, or invading foreign countries with the rhythm of Mongolian music, the same way that Genghis Khan galloped through the prairies.

We stopped by several small Buddhist temples before and after lunch. There was even a temple for horses along with shamanistic idols. The religion in Mongolia is about ninety five percent Buddhism. Strangely enough, their religion is actually more inclined to shamanism than Buddhism. People still go to fortunetellers to ask their fate.

The branches of dead trees are in the middle of rock piles four to five feet high and the blue and white clothes hung on the branches where the Mongolians worship for wealth, longevity and healthy life. Whenever we passed these spots our driver honked for a safe drive from the gods.

It was extremely odd and strange that Pascal and Suke did not tell us the host family's name or whereabouts. It was already a couple of hours after our lunch and close to dinnertime. "Kwang, where are we staying?" I asked with curiosity and concern. "I don't know. Suke made a call to the family. They should be ready for us," was Kwang's answer. "I hope we stay in a house." "I agree," was Kwang's quick response. Surprisingly, Kwang also showed his tiredness and discomfort caused by staying in a Ger hut. "But we have to stay for ten more days in the Ger," he concluded.

Pascal, Susan, Kwang and I were in the Number Two car. Susan heard our conversation half asleep and half awake. "Pascal, where are we staying?" was Susan's grumpy question.

"We do not know yet. Suke is trying to arrange it." This unexpected answer was a great shock. Everybody was quiet. Pascal opened his mouth, "Suke is arranging the host family."

Susan interrupted, "No prearrangement?" You could tell she was not a happy camper at all.

"No. We could not. Families are moving periodically from here to there with their Ger and herds, even if we made arrangements they might not be there, most likely." Again we were quiet with great concern.

"We will have dinner with a family inside the Ger, but we cannot stay long in the family quarters because they have babies who are going to bed in the early evening and they have to take care of their animals." Before Pascal barely finished his sentence, "Pascal, then where will we sleep?" He was interrupted by Susan again. Pascal spoke quietly in order to defuse the uneasy situation. "We put up pop tents and will provide air mattresses and sleeping bags." He did not add it will be cold at night and gave us a strong indication that everything will be okay.

We sat in silence. Now we understood why the sleeping bags and tents were in the back of the cars. My hope for Kwang and I to stay in a hotel or a family's house to enjoy a hot shower was burst like a bubble in the ocean.

Around 4:00 p.m. the wind was raging as we drew closer to the northern part of Mongolia. It was getting colder and windy at night, but the daytime was still warm, so we started to wear layers before we arrived at our unknown destination. By communication with three drivers, Pascal and Suke decided where we would stop. All three cars turned to the right from the so-called main road and crossed to a road-less prairie, and drove through very tiny grasses in the semi-desert.

A white Ger stood very lonely, like a monolith, but about two hundred yards away, horses, cows and goats grazed on the short grass.

Pascal and Suke had a quick conversation with the family, but unfortunately, they were not able to fulfill our requirements. With great disappointment, the three drivers started their engines without knowing how many more miles they had to drive to find a family for us.

About twenty - thirty minutes later two Gers appeared about one hundred yards apart. First Suke approached the family and negotiated. We did not know what the guides negotiated with the family members. They said okay gladly. "Yes." We were all pleased to find a location where we could stay. Of course, especially Pascal and Suke were extremely happy with the arrangement. This moment I am thinking about the fate of homeless people. Before I read "Breaking Night" by Liz Murray I thought that most homeless people are lazy and just won't work for their living. After I read her book my thoughts changed a great deal, and I tried to understand their endless efforts for survival. Just now it seemed that we were homeless, looking for a spot to set up our tents and prepare dinner.

"We will all have lamb for dinner." Pascal's eyes were blinking. It seems a very big deal to him. Unfortunately, Kwang does not eat lamb and was not happy at all. He expected some meat like yak. His concern about meals was a very minor issue. We were glad that we found a place to stay. "We will get a sheep from the meadow and kill him, cook it and will have a really nice dinner," Pascal continued.

Everybody's eyes sparkled with interest regarding killing the animals and having dinner at the same spot.

"When will it be ready for dinner?" Debbie asked quite politely like a lady from London.

"They say by 7:00 p.m.," interrupted Suke. Debbie's concern was about having dinner at 7:00 p.m., by killing the animal and cooking it. It was almost 5:00 p.m. Is that enough time? "In two hours everything will be ready," Pascal answered, "That's what they said." We were all getting hungry and had to believe it.

We put up the pop tents, one tent for two people, put the air in the air mattress and got the sleeping bags ready. The wind was getting stronger and chilly. I grabbed my sleeping bag from our luggage, which we brought from home, which can sustain –5 ^{o}F (-20 ^{o}C) on the ice. "Get yours, Kwang, since we brought our own warm sleeping bags."

"Oh. Mmm. We'll be okay," he hesitated. "Are you sure? Don't regret." I thought I might agitate his feelings. He was stubborn. He did not want to take it out from his luggage. He might need to show me he is a strong macho man on a cold night, or he was too lazy to take the sleeping bag from the bottom of the luggage. I did not know. But regretfully, he did not use his nice warm sleeping bag.

The family Ger had a satellite dish and solar panels for electricity. There was even goat cheese drying on the roof of the Ger. The size of the Ger is the same as we stayed in for several nights, not bigger and not an inch smaller. About two hundred yards away one more Ger stood with enough goat dung spread like black beans on the ground among very short grass on the desert.

Kwang and I went to the small hill to do the facility business in a natural site.

Meanwhile a white sheep came to the Ger on a small white truck. The truck had four wheels, but it looked just like a three wheeled motorcycle with the lower body frame. It's really a very tiny truck. The sheep was quiet on the truck. That sheep would be our dinner tonight.

After we put up the tent, I went to the sheep, which was lying down on the cardboard. It was already in the final stage of dying, "How do you kill him?" I asked Suke in an unpleasant voice.

"Cut the aorta, the big blood vessel," Suke answered easily without any emotion and continued, "That way it is a quick killing and easy for the animal. All Mongolians do it this way."

I thought they would kill the animal by cutting its throat or its stomach. Anyway, it was a really quick, quiet and skillful slaughter.

I came back to the tent, told Kwang about their skillful technique in slaughtering sheep and added it was our dinner. After they peeled the skin from the body very nicely, they cut the sheep piece by piece like the meat at the grocery. Drivers peeled the potatoes and cleaned the onions in two big aluminum pots. They put sheep chops with bones, potatoes, and onions together with fist size rocks into the pots and cooked it for two hours.

Meanwhile Kwang and I strolled around the Ger. Again two hundred yards away to the east side of the camp, flocks of goats, of black and white sheep, and four or five camels mingled with the sheep. When we came back Pascal called us, "Kwang and Kook-Wha, join us for a snack inside the Ger." "Sure." When we went inside, two single beds were along the wall and a small chest between them was locked. Gene asked, "Why is the chest locked?" Suke answered, "The ladies are hiding sweets. The children grab them if it is not locked." "Mmm. It makes sense," Gene commented. Inside the Ger a small TV was on the shelf and another kitchen chest was at the right hand side at the entrance, and between two beds the filtration unit with a cloth filter media was installed with a thirty gallon capacity container for the filtration of vodka.

On the left is mainly a kitchen with large and small pots that hung on the wall and in the process of making goat cheese in a white cloth bag with gravitational methods.

So far during our travel, there were no stoves in our Ger for five to six days, but this family had a stove and the fuel was horse dung and maybe cow too. Because of our sudden visit without any previous arrangement with this family, our drivers were collecting dry dung to cook our dinner. We all sat on the edge of the bed and on very small stools and some people took off their shoes and sat on

91

the vinyl floor. Their three year old daughter was wandering around among us, and a baby was sleeping on the bed.

Fifteen people from our side, including three drivers and three people from the host family were gathered in a tiny space inside the Ger.

The most amazing thing was the fuel of horse dung was very high BTU and we did not have any problem cooking the delicious lamb chops in a short time.

They served us pieces of goat cheese and really sweet, hard candies with warm white goat tea in a soup bowl. It was like warm milk. It had no taste at all and I could not finish it. Then later homemade goat vodka, which was made by using the filtration unit, was served. We were all in a good mood, with nice tea, vodka and goat cheese. I did not drink any vodka, but I was told that it was milder than the Russian brands. The alcohol content was in the range of wine. The cheese was sharp just like a regular cheese. In spite of the loud conversation and laughter spread in the room, the baby slept without any disturbance, once or twice he opened his eyes and went back to sleep again.

Dinner was ready. First from the pot the number two driver, Namhae, took out all the rocks from the pots and passed it one by one. We put the grease and hot rock in our hands and tossed it into both hands alternately, because it was hot, and then passed the plates with the lamb chops with boiled potatoes and onions. With greasy hands, without knives or forks, we had the lamb chops that were warm, and well seasoned. It was absolutely delicious. As I mentioned, fresh food, fresh taste, we could not expect anything fresher than this meal. My curiosity of putting rocks into the pot with lamb chops could not stop asking "Suke, why did you put rocks into the pot?" "It gives it a unique flavor," Suke answered with a smile. "From rocks?" "Yes. It gives it flavor and it is also our tradition." My next question would have been, "How do you create the unique flavor with rocks in the pot?" but I stopped there because he said it was their tradition and I did not feel I should ask him any more questions.

After we finished the meal, we gave gifts to the host family, one bottle of vodka, cucumber pickles and chocolate candies that we bought at the supermarket. Then Suke served the vodka, which we brought in a silver cup from oldest first. In Mongolian tradition, the welcoming gesture is serving vodka or liquor in a silver cup. The cup has a long stem like wine glasses and the upper part of the cup is very shallow like an ice cream cup. Of course, Kwang was served first as the oldest person and next me and so on. Kwang did not eat the lamb chops, but had a good time with the vodka and potatoes with greasy hands.

After dinner we came out to our campsite and danced to the music from the radio in the car and watched the family's activities. The young couple with their daughter herded the goats and sheep in front of the Ger.

The sheep, most of them, were in one place lined up in front of Ger, but four to five ran away and the couple went to bring them back. And made them line up, head to head with each other and started milking. Amazingly they all were quiet until all done. Again all creatures were following the natural rules. I was thrilled about creation and the wonders of nature.

Seven pop tents were set up side-by-side and three cars made a fence to provide protection from the strong wind for our tents.

The full moonlight poured into our tents. I heard Rob snoring, but Sabrina and Raechel continued to talk. I could not sleep. They put the tents just one or two feet away. It was too close.

Kwang started to snore. Somehow I had to sleep. My sleeping bag was so comfortable and warm but I could not sleep. *This is the nomadic life. I have more than enough experience. I need my own warm bed.* I murmured in my mind.

A couple of hours later Kwang woke up and I heard him looking for a windbreaker and sweater. He was cold. I wanted to say, "Kwang, I told you."

In Mongolia we spent the night in tents among sheep, camels and cows under the beautiful moonlight on the vast prairie.

When we came out from the tent it was around 7:00 a.m. and already the sheep left the Ger. They were on the grass. The breakfast was bread and jam, the instant Nescafe coffee and Mongolian warm tea, which I did not like. It's like Apac milk, but they said tea.

Figure 43 Butchered Sheep

Figure 44   Sheep's Hide

Figure 45   Family Dinner inside Ger

Figure 46 Family Dinner

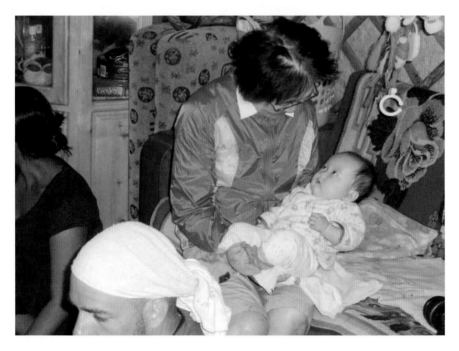

Figure 47 Baby at the Family Dinner

Singing Sands in the Gobi Desert

Mongolia reminds me of leading the nomadic life and the Gobi Desert. Without one inch mistake, I can say Mongolia is a desert. The vast land consists of prairies and bold mountains without any trees or grass in the desert or semi-desert. After many days in Ger camp life we came in front of sand dunes in the Gobi Desert.

At the Sleeping Bear Dunes near Traverse City in Michigan, there are quite a few good-sized sand dunes. When our children were young a couple of times we went there and enjoyed playing with sand and climbed the dunes. The sand dunes in the Gobi Desert are giants compared to the ones in Michigan and are different from the plain and plateau desert in Egypt.

Suddenly, in the prairie the layers of sand mountains were near our Ger camps. We all were stunned at the magnificent natural mystery of a sand dune that is over one hundred miles long with the highest peak reaching above eight hundred meters.

"Wow! Wow! It's beautiful," I exclaimed. I held Kwang's hand tightly while we looked at Pascal's energetic face with a hilarious smile. He said, "We are extremely lucky. The camels are ready for us to go to the sand dune." Before we unloaded our luggage to a Ger camp he checked the availability of camels. At that time he was not sure we could get it on time. "In thirty minutes, as soon as we settle down, we will ride the camels and go to the sand dunes."

The two humped Mongolian camels (Bactrian) were sitting down outside the camp waiting for us with their big eyes wandering around and constantly chewing something in their mouths.

"Pascal (our main guide), this is the second time I am riding a camel. For two hours riding do you think I can handle him?" I explained my concern about a two hour long ride. The first time I rode one was just twenty - thirty minutes at the pyramids in Egypt.

"The camels are tame. No problem. I have not experienced any accidents so far," Pascal assured me. One by one we were in the saddle between two humps with a few words of instruction on how to handle camels.

"Hold tight to the hump or carpet of saddle when the camel stands up. That's it," Suke, the assistant local guide, continued, "After that the camels just follow the leader. One will be in the front and the other one in the back."

"Wow. Wow," Everybody screamed when the camels stood up. It was high, more than six feet from the ground. Luckily nobody fell off.

It was an easy, slow ride. There was no galloping. The trip to the bottom of the dune was about two miles. Occasionally I took a picture of Kwang, with the sand dunes as background.

At the bottom of the dune we all got off the camels and started to climb up the hill. Kwang, Rob from England, Suke, Pascal and I climbed and the rest of the people stayed at the bottom and enjoyed the scenery and played with the sand.

The light yellow, almost white, fine sand made the small hills and also the mountains. We were climbing a sand mountain. One foot forward and one-half foot backward, making big footprints. Even though we climbed zigzag, making our own remarkable traces, it's absolutely difficult to overcome and make it to the top, even if it was not the highest peak of the "Singing Sands".

Finally we made it to the top and found out the sand dune continues to make layers and layers like mountains beyond where we stood. The strong wind created waves of sand, like big seashells with beautiful patterns. By absorbing the beauty of the design of sand, I did not mind the blowing sands getting into my mouth and striking my face. Coming down was much easier and fun and we were jumping down to the bottom. I noticed that our old footprints were already covered by the blowing sand.

We came back again across the prairie with the beautiful sunset with red, orange and white clouds shrouding the sun. It was absolutely stunning scenery, almost beyond my description.

I patted the camel with relief and joy, without falling down from his hump. *Mr. Camel, you did a good job for me.* I patted him again.

With this climbing dunes experience, tomorrow we will climb "Singing Sands" which is the highest peak among the sand dunes, eight hundred fifteen meters.

The next morning after breakfast we drove about thirty minutes from the camp and came at the bottom of the "Singing Sands". Rob, Debbie, Sabrina, Kwang and I joined, of course, two guides, Suke and Pascal, too. Debbie wanted to wander at the bottom and it ended up just Rob, Sabrina, Kwang and I.

At the bottom of the sand dune we stepped on the wet sand and could see the trace of water that flowed. *A trace of water is here in the desert?*

For my comment Suke said, "The rainy season in summer has quite substantial rainfall. It makes an oasis."

"That's very unique, just the bottom of a sand dune," was another comment of mine.

We started to climb. It was getting harder and harder. The zigzag practice did not work well. One foot forward, I made only one quarter foot progress. Kwang wanted to have rests more frequently than before. While resting I could spot the one - two feet tall green reeds from the sand. The leaves were very soft and they seemed very fragile. Suke was right. Even eight hundred meters high up the sand dune, the small green reeds can grow among the wet sand. The wonders of nature astonished me.

Rob passed us and, of course, Pascal did a long time ago. Sabrina, Kwang and I stuck together to try to reach the top. The strong winds made it difficult to continue. It was very hard to keep my eyes open. About a couple hundred meters left from the top Kwang wanted to stop. I felt the same. "Sabrina, you go ahead. We will stay here and rest. Enjoy the sand."

We could see the Land Cruiser down in the prairie like a small matchbox. For a few moments more we enjoyed looking at the scenery, but a strong wind kept blowing sand in my ears, mouth and camera. However, Kwang and I could hear the musical sounds. It's hard to describe the sounds that I was hearing, but it was rhythmic and pleasant sounds.

"Ah, ah. This is the "Singing Sands", Kwang, can you hear?" "Yes. Yes," It sounds like an orchestra without any harmony," Kwang commented.

"Listen carefully, Kwang. It might be the symphony playing Beethoven." We laughed at our imagination. "Beethoven symphony," I added.

"Wait a minute, your imagination is too far off from the realistic," Kwang criticized my wild, unbelievable imagination, but we heard some sounds.

I have searched the "Singing Sands," from Wikipedia:

"The name for the region in Mongolia is Hongory Els, meaning "Singing Sands." It refers to noise made by sand grains as they pass over each other when wind moves them across the surface of the dunes. Unlike most sand particles, which are coarse and irregular, the particles of the Singing Sands are round and smooth. In dry weather conditions, these particles of sand rub against each other, creating an eerie musical sound.

Importantly, there are still scientific controversies on the details of the singing sand mechanism. It has been proposed that the sound frequency is controlled by the shear rate. Others have suggested that the frequency of vibration is related to the thickness of the dry surface layers of sand. The sound waves bounce back and forth between the surface of the dune and the surface of the moist layer creating a resonance that increases the sound's volume."

We were listening to the music of the "Singing Sands" from Bach, Beethoven and Brahms with great appreciation, pretending that we were in Orchestra Hall.

Figure 48 Gobi Dessert

Figure 49 Horseback Ride

EUROPE

Checkpoint Charlie

For a pre-trip of our Eastern Europe tour, Kwang and I spent three nights and four days in the eastern part of Berlin that was under the communist regime twenty years ago. July 2010 was a record breaking sizzling hot summer in East Berlin.

It was unavoidable to ask pedestrians several times for the location of "Checkpoint Charlie", even if Kwang had clearly marked the spot on the map before we left the hotel. The reason for the difficulties in finding Checkpoint Charlie was the building was scaled down to one quarter and stood in the middle of the street.

I looked for a bigger building with a several layers of thick wire fences around it, like in the movies and the news. Contrary to my imagination, one side of the barracks is Russian and the other one was American, connected with one wall. It was very small, like a doghouse on the street.

"Take a pose with the guards." Kwang ordered me, as usual, to pose for a Kodak moment. "Yes", I answered and I ran to the Russian guards who were short and wearing the typical Russian green uniform and a rectangular cap with one big star in the front. "Two Euro per picture taken," the two guards warned us even before I approached them, with strong German accent.

It was very rude, unacceptable behavior. Absolutely I could not go near the barracks. As soon as I stepped down from the sidewalk into the middle of the road, they shouted again to stop Kwang from taking a picture of the street scene because they saw his huge Kodak camera.

Hmm. €2 is $3. It is ridiculous. I mumbled and tried to behave myself without saying anything else. In Europe almost everywhere they asked us for money, money, money, even for restrooms. It seems they have gold rush fever through American tourists.

Kwang said in Korean, "No way we should pay to take a picture of the barracks with the guards." Then he continued in Korean, "Kook-Wha, turn around, don't leave there. I will take a picture." Then he took out the huge telephoto lens and he did what he wanted. With an awkward and uncomfortable feeling at this location, we went around to the American side. Two guards wearing green uniforms with the "M P" mark on the white helmets and the American flag on their left chest on their uniforms, stood in front of the small door at the barracks, and were talking about something while looking at the street. Kwang and I did not attempt to approach them to take pictures, because they were just model guards for the American side.

Since 1989 after the Berlin Wall came down, East Berlin became a capitalistic society. It has already been over twenty years. I thought they had a smooth transition from a communist to a capitalistic society, but the concept of monetary and material rewards was extremely greedy. I hope they can exercise this in an appropriate way. We are all saying, "There is no free lunch".

We work hard to achieve our goals whatever they might be, but €2 for a picture is too easy money and greedy.

Kwang and I were quietly strolling on the street with bitter feelings and sort of anger. My whole life I have hated to see some people take advantage of others, or lazy, or everything comes easily to their hands for a comfortable life. Another thought came into my mind, these are worldwide trends pursuing easy money? In our chemical engineering course we learned the material balance of input and output. The material values were unbalanced at Checkpoint Charlie.

A hundred yards away from the barracks of Checkpoint Charlie on the northern side was a two story building which was the museum of Checkpoint Charlie and on the southern side, both sides of the street had wooden fence about two and one-half meters high with many historical pictures of the Berlin Wall, from the starting point of construction to 1989 when it was taken down.

Ronald Reagan's famous speech, "Mr. Gorbachev, tear down this wall" and John F. Kennedy in 1963 "Ich bin ein Berliner" were on the posts.

Now the Berlin Wall remains just small pieces for tourism and the posters of its Wall on the fence. Red brick marks remain at the location of the Berlin Wall on the street, serving as landmarks for remaining historical evidence.

Germany became united as one nation from East and West twenty-one years ago. Korea has been divided into North and South Korea for sixty five years, since 1945 after World War II. Two different ideologies against each other divided by the DMZ (demilitarized zone). The North Korean soldiers are pointing their cannon or guns at the South and vice versa. Why is it so difficult for the Korean peninsula to become united?

The Berlin Wall was taken down and Checkpoint Charlie is gone but the DMZ in Korea still exists and is waiting to disappear as soon as possible by unification.

Figure 50 Check Point Charlie

Figure 51   Checkpoint Charlie

Figure 52   Check Point Charlie

Wieliczka Salt Mine

We arrived at the Wieliczka Salt Mine near Krakow, Poland, a UNESCO heritage site, in the late afternoon in July 2010. The tour guide for Eastern Europe, Helena, was born and grew up in Warsaw, Poland. She warned us, "We have to go through about four hundred wooden steps down. Anybody who is not comfortable with that many steps in this salt mine can wait at the souvenir shop which is located across the street from the main entrance to the salt mine. Our tour will be over in about two or two and one-half hours. Afterwards we will have an authentic Polish dinner at the local restaurant".

Bill from California is over seventy five years old and still working as a substitute teacher in elementary school, and Joe from New Jersey who just retired from working in the medical field, decided to wait at the souvenir shop. Bill, who has a knee problem, carried his own small chair all the time, which was a combination of sticks that became a small chair when he unfolded it.

A red roofed, small, white walled building stands on the hillside, where the salt mine entrance is located. "Inside the mine it is cold. Does everybody have a jacket or a sweater?" Helena asked us, in quite energetic and demanding tones, rather than her normal soft one.

From the day we arrived in Berlin we had sizzling hot weather. It lasted for about seven days. The shade under the trees was an absolute must during our walk. Until this afternoon's overcast sky, everybody had a hard time avoiding the heat and longed for the water bottles and cooler spots. The brochure for Eastern Europe indicates that the average temperature in July is 70 – 75 °F. The highest temperature is 85 °F, but all last week the temperature was above 90 °F during the day. Most of us in our group had not prepared our travel gear for this hot weather.

"Are the stairs safe? How deep are we going down?" George from Virginia Beach, Virginia asked.

Helena was quiet, then after a few minutes, "The stairs are sturdy, but the wood may be slippery when they are wet, be careful. We are going down about one hundred meters by elevator and after that going down to four hundred meters underground by the stairs. Everybody was quiet at the astonishing number of "four hundred meters".

Helena did not stop and continued to summarize what we would see, "You will see fantastic sculptures carved by the miners."

"All made from rock salt?" Kwang asked.

This was not normal for him. He is usually quiet almost everywhere, all the time. Sometimes when I am really upset I tell him, "Kwang, speak up if you have a mouth. When you die, you will never speak again, so say what you have in mind at the moment". He just grinned and walked away from me, and this made me even angrier at him.

"Yes. All made from rock salt by amateur miners," she answered in a lower voice than before and at the same time we saw the uniformed guide approaching us wearing a hard white hat as a miner.

"Grand Circle Group, my name is Joseph and I am your guide, please follow me and stick together. If you get lost here inside the mine you will never survive to find the exit." From his gestures and the way he talked to us, I immediately understood that it comes from his bountiful experience, not only as a guide in the salt mine, but also from speaking with such fluent English. I wanted to tell him that his English is impeccable.

We took an elevator that only holds nine people. Like a seesaw game the elevator was operating from gravity, such as one is up and one is down and the most unique thing was that it did not have solid walls. The wall panels were steel that had lots of small holes. I could hear voices from the other elevators. This elevator reached sixty four meters from the ground and from there we descended about four hundred steps on wooden stairs and were about three hundred fifty meters deep.

We were told the Wieliczka Salt Mine is two hundred miles long. We only toured about one percent of it, about two miles for about two hours. As soon as we left the elevator there is the Janowice chamber, which illustrated the legend of the discovery of rock salt in the thirteenth century. A miner gave Kinga, daughter of the Hungarian King, a block of salt and an engagement ring. Then we passed the corridor, approximately seven ft. high, four to five feet wide. The floor, walls and ceiling are made from rock salt.

I could see the graffiti in Polish with small pictures carved on the wall. I was beside or behind the guide all the time, in order not to miss his explanations.

At ten – twenty meter intervals, there was a door which closes the connection to the next corridors.

A lady from California asked from far behind at the end of our group, "How many doors total in this mine?"

Joseph did not hear her and he continued his explanation. I repeated her question to him. "Joseph, why are there so many doors between corridors, and how many are there?"

"Ah, ah, good question. There are about nineteen to protect from explosion, fire and for containment." Joseph's hesitation at the numbers indicated that there are many more doors, but he only counted the tourist area.

At least a couple of times a day Joseph repeated this tour. He was acting like a clock. At a certain point he knew the duration of time spent. The big surprise for us was his punctuality and the numbers he remembered, I was beside him all the time and asked him most of the questions, even though I read the information Kwang prepared from Wikipedia.

"Why did the salt mine close down?" I expected his answer to be 'more than economical feasibility', but Joseph gave me the same answer written in the Wikipedia. However, he added, "We exported the salt to a radius of over two hundred miles to several countries".

110

The next corridor was so different than the others, with lumber. "Joseph, why lumber and why white paint?" I asked.

"Excellent question, listen our group, the lumber keeps a constant temperature killing bacteria and fungus growth and the white paint gives more light reflection. Of course, inside the mine it is about $54 - 57\ ^\circ$F constantly." I could not make sense of it at all, lumber protecting against bacteria and fungus growth, but he explained it based on his experience and facts.

This is the first time in my life inside not only a salt mine, but any mine. I had imagined a dirty, narrow and dark coal mine. But, in contrast, the floor was clean like my kitchen with dark gray rock salt. Walls also like a gray wallpaper with abstract design. I could not resist tasting the rock salt and rubbed it with my index finger and put it in my mouth. It was not like our table salt, but a slight salty flavor.

Um, it is not really salty. I echoed to myself.

Section by section displayed the old equipment such as pulleys, centrifuges and cleaning stations, and the small water channels were still running down to the bottom of the mine.

"Wow. Wow." Everyone said in chorus when we saw the display of a life-sized horse statue and a man working in the mine. "Wow, Joseph, how did they bring a horse or cow inside the mine to work in the dark?"

"It was not dark, there was light and also, the animals work for ten months and get two months vacation outside the mine. Surprisingly they did not go blind," he answered quickly. Everybody seemed to believe his comments, and he continued, "We have a health chamber inside the mine. People are recovering in this chamber from chronic diseases. If you stay inside the mine's facility for a couple of hours a day for a couple of weeks, arthritis gets better and especially women's skin gets smooth and maybe the wrinkles disappear".

Everybody burst into laughter.

Joseph assured us, "It's true, we have a health chamber in the mine, as I mentioned before".

My thoughts stretched out to the chemistry of salt which consists of Sodium and Chloride. *How can Sodium Chloride improve arthritis and other diseases and especially smooth out the skin?* My imagination did not stop. *Maybe it is the material balance of Sodium Chloride and other minerals in our bodies?* I asked myself.

We continued down onto the wooden steps to descend to the bottom. These wooden stairs are at least three feet wide and have about four foot high protective railings on both sides but the old adjacent stairs made of rock salt made an appearance. Amazingly, they were only one foot wide and had no railing. Miners would carry a load of about forty pounds up and down these narrow stairs, even when the stairs were wet. "Unfortunately, numerous accidents happened", Joseph sighed.

I told Kwang, "The old miners had endurance, were hard working and confronted the threat and fear of accidents. We are living in the world having great technological benefits".

"Sure," was his short answer.

Several times we stopped by the significant sculptures, such as Jozef Pilsudski's sculpture in his chamber. Attached to this chamber, there is a small lake inside of the mine. We were told that Jozef Pilsudski was an important man in Polish history for regaining its independence in 1918 from the Russian, Austrian and Prussian/German partition.

Joseph was getting more energetic, and in contrast, our group was getting more exhausted. But I was the exception. My energy level was upbeat. I was always beside Joseph and making notes of what he told us.

When we came down to the famous "Chapel of St. Kinga" one-half of our members were lagging behind and struggled to finish the last part of approximately four hundred stairs. Joseph announced at the Chapel, "You can look around at the sculptures for about ten minutes. These sculptures were made by three miners, two brothers and one of their friends. They were amateurs and without any formal training in art or sculpture. They did this either before or after their main job".

After a few minutes of quiet was gone, I asked, "Rock salt does not melt with rainwater?" but he ignored my question. This was quite a rational and serious question for me, because salt should be dissolved into water. Maybe I was too curious and that's the reason he started to ignore me. In this case Kwang would usually add some criticism, such as, "Be quiet", or "No more questions", but surprisingly, this time he did not say anything.

Joseph recited quickly about several sculptures on the walls, "Twelve year old Jesus teaching in the Temple, The Last Supper and the most recent one, a 1999 statue of Pope John Paul II". Joseph ended his recital, "Please, look at the sculptures. They are amazing things from amateur talent. In ten minutes let's meet at the corner of the concession stand".

"Ten minutes? How can we see all the sculptures?" the lady from California complained.

"We need ten additional minutes. Let's meet after twenty minutes," I added, getting courage from her suggestion.

"Then in twenty minutes at the concession stand. If you are one minute late, we will leave", Joseph's stern order echoed on the ceiling and he continued, "If you lose the group, you will never find the mine exit". Then he left us at the concession stand for a drink.

"Whew, whew, Kwang, let me sit down for a few minutes. My feet feel like stones that weigh a ton." At our release from Joseph's time machine (our schedule), I felt that the soles of my feet were about to burst into flames.

"You can sit down for a minute. I will take pictures. Twenty minutes is not enough time for looking at all the sculpture and taking pictures," with this quick comment, Kwang disappeared. I found a small chair beside the concession stand and sat down and looked around the hall. It was hard to guess the size of the hall but maybe at least ten thousand square feet adding to the character of the space is its high ceilings. Sculptures were all around the walls and huge white chandeliers dangled from the ceiling. Of course, they were made of rock salt.

Twenty minutes is not enough to absorb all these jewels. I talked to myself and started to walk and read the titles.

"Twelve year old Jesus teaching in the Temple"; facing Jesus there were old men with long beards with hats. By sitting in front of Jesus, they were accepting His teaching. The amazing details of the sculpture made it seem carved in wood instead of gray rock salt.

Jesus' crucifixion, The Last Supper, and the Miracle of Cana of Galilee were carved by a miner sculptor, Antoni Wyrodek. The Last Supper was an exact copy of Leonardo Da Vinci's fresco. The only exception is the gray color. I did a deep bow to the wonders of nature when I was in the Galapagos Islands and Antarctica, but I had to bow more deeply to this astonishing human talent and achievement.

"Kwang, look at that chandelier. They seem to be white crystal, but is really rock salt," I screamed at the surprisingly beautiful crystal chandelier. Kwang just nodded and was busy taking its picture from several different angles.

The statue of Pope John Paul II was one of the most amazing, especially because of the nearby statue of a little Polish boy who is admiring the Holy Father. He was a hero among the Polish people, like Jozef Pilsudski.

We came out to a small lake in the Jozef Pilsudski chamber which has thirty three percent salt content, so that an object cannot sink. This is a similar environment to the Dead Sea. On the way out of the mine was the statue of Johann Wolfgang von Goethe and other sculptures that were created by modern artists.

Joseph did not forget his commercial and advertised, "The chapel of St. Kinga is used for weddings and private parties".

Joe from New Jersey was curious, "How far ahead do we have to make reservations?"

"It depends on how busy the hall is and depends on the number of people," Joseph did not give a clear answer.

We took the same elevator to get back to the original entrance. It took less than a minute and we arrived at the surface from four hundred meters deep.

Joseph did not forget one more thing and almost recited the list of celebrity visitors' names, including famous poets, musicians, and politicians, including President Bill Clinton.

"Wow. He did not miss anybody from his list," I told Kwang.

"No, he did an absolutely great job".

"I was totally intoxicated by his explanation about the mining and the sculptures," I expressed my total satisfaction with our guide.

"Yes. It was good," once again a short comment from Kwang.

Still, drizzling raindrops landed on my head and dusk surrounded the small entrance to the rock salt mine building.

By completing the tour, we felt we had earned an authentic Polish dinner at a local restaurant.

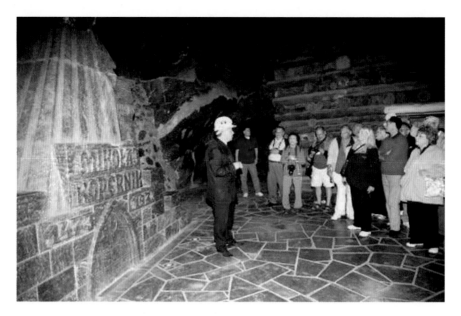

Figure 53 Inside Salt Mine

Figure 54 Last Supper made of Salt

Figure 55 Virgin Mary

Figure 56 Goethe

Figure 57 Salt Warrior

Cruise on the Rhine River with the Lorelei

I completely put the Detroit auto industry's gloomy events from my mind and I was absolutely absorbed into a fantastic dream about the beautiful old castles and the legendary Lorelei on the Rhine River.

We arrived in Amsterdam, Netherlands at dawn on a July morning that was a little chilly. Wearing a short sleeve T-shirt made me shiver and I put my hands into the middle of my chest from force of habit. Quickly I took a light windbreaker from my backpack and even put the hood on my head. Amsterdam is notorious as a damp city.

The Rhine River cruise was from Amsterdam to Vienna. We checked into the ship "Adajeo" for our fourteen day floating hotel and dashed out onto the street and headed towards downtown Amsterdam.

The Adajeo is about thirty yards long and ten yards wide and has a three story deck with about two hundred guest rooms, formal dining room, reception area and lobby that can also be used as a conference room and upper deck for outdoor activities. The space is well organized. In the small kitchen their skilled cooks provided the most delicious meals in the world with beautiful presentations for two hundred people.

The lobby has a piano and a small mini-bar serving alcohol, soft drinks; and coffee and tea is available self –service twenty four hours. It can hold about two hundred people easily for talent shows, and a captain's welcoming or farewell reception. It was adequately sized with a small dance floor in the middle.

Amsterdam means canals, windmills, x-rated streets, the Anne Frank and the Van Gogh Museums. A detailed city map from the boat did not help us find the x-rated area to satisfy Kwang's curiosity. By asking for directions a couple of times we finally arrived at the street which Kwang was looking forward to seeing.

Several two or three story old buildings have signs for restaurants as bar and grill. People were busy preparing tables and chairs for lunch. The neon signs were blinking on the windows. Nothing was unusual or exciting. "Too bad, Kwang," I teased him. He was quiet. "It is quite different than we heard." Still silence. "Yeah, it is different". The activities were totally dead in the daytime. It was a very short street (about thirty meters) and it should have more areas which we did not know. I was told that the women involved in this business have multi-nationalities. Around noontime was not fit for a business deal.

"What a disappointment for Kwang!!! He did not get to see any girls!!!" I mentioned to him again.

Our next stop would be the Anne Frank Museum. On the way to the museum, I bought a couple of small wooden shoes which are symbols of the Netherlands at one of many souvenir shops.

The bicycles are everywhere, maybe more than in China, and they have top priority riding on the streets at full speed, in contrast to pedestrians having top priority in the USA. There are separate bicycle routes next to the lanes of cars even with traffic lights for the bicycles only. Hundreds of bicycles flew down the streets at incredible speed. It was a spectacular scene when thousands of bicycles were parked in a huge parking lot.

The other important transportation tools, like bicycles, are the boats on the canals in Amsterdam. Small and large boats loaded with produce and other items were busy passing each other in the canals. The floating residential houseboats on the canals have television antennas stuck out from the roofs and beautiful summer flowers were blooming in pots hanging near the windows. Bedroom curtains were open and dining tables showed through the windows. Many decks had elegant garden furniture and evergreen plants in pots. Later I heard from the guide that these houseboats are in the range of five hundred thousand dollars to one million dollars.

With unexpected distractions from heading to the Anne Frank Museum, I spent more than an hour at the canals with the desire to rent one of them just for one summer.

Again we crossed over several small bridges over the canals and finally came to the street where the Anne Frank Museum is located. It was already late afternoon when we approached. I was totally exhausted from a couple of hours walking on the mostly cobbled streets and, moreover, the lack of sleep the night before our departure from Detroit. I was looking for a bench to grab a couple minute's rest. Kwang asked again for directions to the Anne Frank Museum. This time he interrupted a lady in a flower shop on the street. "There. It is a couple of blocks away." She showed us the direction with her chin. She had a heavy accent and beautiful long eyelashes. Then she returned her attention to her new customer.

We thought the museum would be a huge building, but it was only a two or three story small black building with long lines of people waiting to enter the museum, actually, it was a house. We were thirty to forty minutes walking distance from the Adajeo. We did not have time to wait to enter the museum.

My disappointment was much greater than Kwang's x-rated street. My eyes were getting warm and my feet and arms lost all strength. "We will be back here sometime", Kwang told me very quietly and tried to comfort me. "Right. We will be back?" It was absolutely my fault. Why was I so excited about the houseboats in the canals that I spent such a long time there?

We arrived at the Adajeo about ten minutes before embarking at 4:00 p.m. One hundred sixty-four passengers were not young people. Their average ages were seventy years old, if my guess was right. Very few people were still working, either as part-time or as consultants, and most of them were retired schoolteachers or college professors with some kind of family ties with Germany, such as a soldier's participation in WW II, relatives that are still in Germany, or parents or grandparents that came to the U.S. as immigrants.

The Adajeo left Amsterdam and sailed through the night and we toured the next big cities, Cologne, Koblenz, Heidelburg, Nuremberg, Weltberg, Regensburg and ended in Vienna, Austria.

After breakfast or lunch, we disembarked at the cities and had excursions to famous cathedrals, churches, museums and sites of big events to observe cultural and historical differences in each city. Every evening there was a short briefing for the next day's excursion before a formal four course dinner.

Eighty to ninety percent of the big cities in Germany were totally destroyed by air raids during World War II. With the German's diligent hard work all the cities were rebuilt. For whatever reason, a few cities, such as Bamberg and Wurzburg, escaped the bombing of World War II and are designated as "UNESCO Heritage Sites".

When we passed the Lorelei, we stayed on the boat without excursions in the cities.

The farm houses had red roofs and white walls, and made mosaics on the green vineyards on the hills along the riverbank. Occasionally a couple of white swans were floating near the banks of the Rhine but I never saw anyone working in the farms or vineyards. The Rhine River has heavy traffic, with passenger boats and cargo ships, carrying coal, produce, automobiles and almost everything you could name. Before the widening and the construction of the Rhine River canals and locks, this transportation was done via railroads, but that took more time than the river.

On the cargo ships, there are living quarters over the engine compartment with windows covered with curtains. Baby cribs and playpens were seen through the windows. Also, they often carry one or two small cars for city transportation when they dock the ships at ports. When we saw a small swing set on the deck of a coal cargo ship, we all screamed at once, "Look at the swing set". The ship carried a beautiful family, along with the coal.

Through the Adajeo's large windows in the lobby we watched a couple of fishermen on the riverbank and the small campgrounds with a tiny tent with two people. But, occasionally we saw large campgrounds with several German flags on the camper roofs. The captain announced, "We are approaching the beautiful

Lorelei who flirts with everybody. She is especially known for taking many sailors' lives. She will be on your left in five minutes."

We all rushed to the left side windows and then the Rhine River started curving and almost zigzagging. "Our captain has over ten years experience on the Rhine River. We are safe, but you never know. The captain may lose consciousness, because of the Lorelei's beauty," the guide continued. "Please hold onto your boat tightly." "Here we are at the middle of the mountain at the bank of the river and the small Lorelei is flirting with you." The captain directed the location and everybody was ready with cameras and had their eyes focused on the mountain for the Lorelei.

Kwang said, "there", then he clicked his camera. I was ready with mine, but I could not find it. "Darn! Where? Where?" I screamed. But the boat had already turned the corner. I could not see it. This has happened many times. Kwang could see the objects and observe the very valuable landmarks, but I could not see them. The reality … my eyesight is better than his. He wore thick eyeglasses before he had cataract surgery. When I saw his picture later, the Lorelei was on the small rock almost hiding among the leaves of trees.

The afternoon cruise was quite relaxing, no lectures and no demonstrations. The castles on the cliffs with forts are waiting for new owners. Each castle has its own unique characteristics, depending on the period of construction. It was just post card scenery.

With tons of coffee I started to write in my journal. Christina from California came to me and started a conversation, "What are you writing? Are you a journalist or a writer?"

"Um, um, no. I am an engineer."

"Oh. My husband, Jim, is an engineer."

"Oh, yeah. What kind?" I showed some interest.

"He is a seismic engineer. Jim goes all over the world. He went to Vietnam to survey the ocean for oil."

"Very interesting. I am a chemical engineer."

"Wow. I am a homemaker. I thought you were a kind of journalist or writer, because you take notes about whatever the guide says."

"Yes. I take notes. It is just a habit." In my mind, I just said *I am trying to be a writer*.

The next morning there was a glass blowing demonstration on the boat from the local factory. The first year in the chemistry lab at the engineering college the instructor taught us the most important tricks, such as methods for using Bunsen burners, collecting spilled mercury on the lab bench and making our own glassware, mostly connecting tubes, avoiding burning our fingers. The gentleman from the glass factory demonstrated as a magician and delicately handled the glassware, making wine glasses from glass tubes. I was amazed by his skill, because I had relied on my lab partner for glass-working, and that was more than fifty years ago. Most women screamed "wow", when he made a beautiful small vase from a tinted glass tube.

Beer in Germany, most of us would remember the movie scene of the students at the University of Heidelberg drinking beer with large beer mugs and dancing and swinging their arms with the mugs, "drink, drink, drink." But in recent days they served beer in long narrow tall glasses, like everywhere else.

Each town has their own small brewery with pride in its own taste and a unique brand name. One town has smoked beer. The smell and taste is like smoked barbeque smell. Almost everybody ordered a small jug of smoked beer and tasted it on the small bench on the side street. "It has a real smoked barbecue smell. Ha, Ha." John from Kentucky was laughing with beer bubbles on his mouth. We were told in the US that in Germany beer is cheaper than water. So we should drink beer instead of water. There are hundreds of varieties of beer available in each town, but water was still cheaper than beer.

Most of the guests on board, and Kwang was no exception, were enjoying the wine and beer at dinner with no limits on service. Vineyards are spread around the hills along the Rhine River to produce ninety percent white wine and only ten percent red. For a couple of days Kwang was drunk from the free wine. He could not watch the movies. The ship showed us two movies every day on the TV inside the cabins for our entertainment, mostly classics, such as "The Sound of Music" or "Giant".

Beer and wine for Kwang, for me it was the famous hand woven linen in Germany. I did not realize the time went so fast in linen shops, I spent too much time in the shops and almost missed the designated departure time. Of course, Kwang was so upset and his eyes were getting smaller than before and it was hard to open them. "People are waiting for you," he yelled at me with a lowered voice to avoid being heard by the other people listening. I shrugged my shoulders and joined the group, showing I was not late and was on time. I bought several bookmarks made of linen. The names of German cities were embroidered on them. Table cloths, pillow cases and others are too expensive for my budget and also, I thought in the US, I can buy it cheaper than here "on sale". Of course, they are not the same quality as in Germany.

We stopped by several cities during our fourteen day cruise. The night before Nuremberg we were shown a documentary and slides about Germany ... past, present and future, including the story of the Nuremberg trials by a German historian in the reception hall. I pitied myself for my ignorance of world history. It seemed that I never heard about it or I totally forgot the story or I wanted to forget it? Anyway, the Nuremberg trials were not in my mind. Today, Germans are struggling and working hard to build a respectable society from the lessons learned from the past Nazi era. In the schools they are teaching the pupils about World War II, Nazis' behavior and respect for human rights and life and building a beautiful society for the future. No one on the boat wants any more examples like the Nazis. We exchanged "good night" to each other with unusually solemn and quiet greetings.

126

After we got back to our cabin, we watched "Judgment at Nuremberg" with Montgomery Clift, Spencer Tracy, Richard Widmark, Maximilian Schell, Burt Lancaster, Judy Garland and Marlene Dietrich, among others. The image of incredible defense from Maximilian Schell as a lawyer for the Nazi criminals and calm and intelligent judge, Spencer Tracy, were put into my brain. I want to bed with the slight rocking of the boat. Kwang was snoring a long time ago with his excessive wine.

The next morning we did a Nuremberg city tour and went to the grounds where Hitler made a historical speech. We saw the document center just outside of the building.

During our fourteen day cruise from Amsterdam to Vienna, we passed sixty nine locks, especially the locks on the Danube and the Rhine ... the height is eighty one feet. The boat and the lock space is quite a tight fit, so there was not much space through the locks. The captain was maneuvering mystically, precisely through the locks. The lock design especially at the Danube and the Rhine is proof of the highest German engineering technology in the world.

We disembarked in Vienna and returned home.

Figure 58 Along Rhine River

Figure 59 Along Rhine River

Figure 60 Along Rhine River

Figure 61 Loreley In Rhine River

Breakfast in Vienna

In spring 2009, when I left Detroit it was 68 °F with bountiful sunshine on my back. I did not need any coat, just a turtleneck was more than enough. Actually, I forgot to bring a coat and went back home on the way to the airport and took one light spring jacket.

I had a very comfortable flight to Amsterdam and arrived at the airport at 5:30 a.m. with the dawn. I only had an hour layover time to Vienna. The terminal to Vienna was almost thirty minutes away from my arrival terminal from Detroit. The worst thing was that I had to pass through immigration.

There are two sections: one for European passports and the other one for all passports. The line was ridiculously long for all passports. I was frustrated and worried about missing the flight to Vienna. My frustration became anxiety and I started to be agitated. I warned myself, *You'd better behave yourself. Hey, Kook-Wha, the sky will not fall down.* But my anxiety showed on my face and it was almost burning. An additional concern was, even if I made it, how about my luggage?

Only thirty minutes left and luckily, the line was getting shorter and shorter. A man was being held at the window at immigration for at least five minutes and then another officer came and took him away to the main office. Normally it took only one or two minutes. I asked the person who was controlling the lines whether I could make my connection within twenty five minutes. The person said, "You can make it. Don't worry." Now I am starting to sweat. My blood pressure was up. My head was getting heavier and I felt a little dizzy. *Hey, why are you so nervous? You* can take the next flight, stupid, somebody in my mind reminded me. *Yes. Right. There is no reason to raise your blood pressure.*

Finally it was my turn. The officer asked me, "What is the purpose of this trip?" "It is business, for a conference." My answer was short. He did not look at me. He flipped over my thick passport with many stamps from different countries. "What kind of conference?" "Nanotechnology." He did not say anything else; he just passed me my passport. It took me just less than one minute. I ran to the gate holding my breath. Luckily several people were ahead of me waiting to board. Maybe nanotechnology is a new word for him.

The signs in the Vienna airport were not clear. I had to ask a couple of times about the location for baggage claim. The last person told me, "Just follow the pictures of baggage" in a hostile tone. Oh, yes, I was blind! I did not notice the pictures on the board and was just looking for the letters "baggage claim". With such a short layover time, my bag came in the first round. *Mmm, the priority tag on the luggage was working this time*. I said to myself with relief.

Breakfast - The first day

The conference office designates several hotels for attendees. The Hotel Capri where I stayed is located the furthest distance from Tech Gate where the conference was held.

The next morning I went down to the breakfast room on the second floor. Several people were having breakfast very quietly in the room. On the serving counter there was a coffee pot, hot water, juices (mangoes, oranges and apples). There was milk for cereal and several kinds of breads, cheeses (Britto, American and Swiss) and cold cuts (ham, turkey, salami) and fresh fruit (bananas, apples, pears and kiwi), with sliced vegetables (cucumber, peppers and tomatoes) and boiled eggs. Boiled eggs, milk and sliced cucumber is perfect for my breakfast.

I looked around the tables and wondered if anybody came for the conference. The couple across my table looked like tourists. At the northeast corner a young man was having breakfast by himself with his head down to the plate and eating as though he had been starved for several days. I was sure that he had come for the conference and I wanted to ask him whether we could go to the Tech Gate together, but he quickly left the room before I had a chance to ask. A young group came in and sat at a long table and they seemed to wait for a couple of more people. When I approached the counter to get bread an African lady mentioned, "Your pants have a white spot. Maybe you rubbed your pants on the wall". Covered with embarrassment, I started dusting my pants off without thinking that I might make the tiny breakfast room dusty. "Thank you." Then I discontinued the conversation with her. My embarrassment made me stop searching for attendees for the conference. I quickly grabbed a coffee mug and sweet roll and took my seat. The coffee and sweet roll were delicious and smoothed out the strong European coffee. A few minutes later a young Chinese guy came in with a crew cut. He was about five feet four inches, short, about thirty years old wearing an old sweater with cheap polymer fabric. His serious expression and his hairstyle proclaimed that his previous profession was a soldier in the Red army. My assurance that he would be attending the conference led me to approach him without hesitation.

As soon as he put his plate on the table, I asked him, "Are you attending the nanotechnology conference?" With his eyes becoming as large as golf balls, he answered, "Yes". Then he almost asked me, "So what?" I told him, "I am attending too. Can we go together?" I asked him straightforward without any long explanation. "Sure," he said while his expression questioned why I am asking if we can go together. "Meet me at 9:00 a.m. in the lobby" I demanded. "Yes." With this short answer he left the room. With great relief, I could start to enjoy my breakfast.

I was so nervous going to a new place alone because almost everywhere we go, Kwang gets all the directions and maps of subway lines. I just followed him. When I go to a conference myself, usually the conference location is at the same hotel where I was staying. There is no hassle to be at the conference location. To reduce expenses I stayed in an €92/night hotel instead of an €132/night attached to the Tech Gate.

I spent the whole day with Mr. Guo, at the subway, the conference and the tour at AC^{2}T Research GmbH, which is one of the biggest Tribology centers in Europe.

Breakfast – the second day – with Mr. Guo

I sat down across from Mr. Guo in the middle of the dining room at a table for two people. "Can we walk to Tech Gate today?" I opened the conversation. "It is snowing," Mr. Guo responded. "Is it really?" I opened the sheer curtain. "Oh, wow. It is snowing heavily but it is not staying on the ground." While holding the curtain and looking down on the ground I exclaimed about the snow in Vienna in March. "This afternoon I cannot. I have to make a presentation," Mr. Guo continued. "Today we can take the subway and tomorrow, we walk to the Tech gate," I suggested.

We exchanged formal greetings and introduced ourselves for the first time. I told him about my retirement three years ago and now I am working as a consultant for the same company. Before retirement I did not have time to do any basic research for the company. Also, at the present time nanotechnology cannot be applied directly to our business but I am preparing for the future and added, it is a fascinating field.

He was a Ph.D. candidate at a university in Belgium. His research was in a very specific narrow area, even in nanotechnology. He lived in Belgium with his wife. "I am originally from Xian, China." "I know Xian with underground soldiers," I interrupted him. "I was there two years ago on the way to the Yellow Mountain."

"What language do they speak in Belgium?" I continued. "French." His answer was short again. "What about English?" "At school we use English, but most of the people speak French." "It must be quite confusing for you … Chinese, French, and English."

"Yes." For a minute he was quiet, then he continued, "My wife was a translator in Japanese in China. There is not much opportunity for her in Belgium." He indicated indirectly his wife's talent with languages.

He was going back to China to teach at the university. "One more year left." His relief showed on his face that he only has one more year left of school. "How about moving to the USA or to Germany after you get your degree? We need scientists in nanotechnology." He hesitated for a few minutes. "No. I will go back to China." It was an unexpected and strong answer. I had no words against his patriotic mind towards China. I was shown by him that my suggestion was inadequate.

We were in the same situation. After I graduated from college I wanted to go back to Korea to teach advanced technology at the university but the situation changed after graduation. We had the experience of the convenience and the comfortable life in the USA and the children started school. It was harder to go back to Korea. I was envious of his ambition and goals for his country as a young scientist.

It was still snowing hard.

"I have to change my clothes. See you in the lobby at 8:30 a.m." As I left the table, he was drinking the last sip of his coffee.

Breakfast - the third day – with Mr. Koshi Adachi from Japan

I woke up late and watched a little bit of CNN about AIG's new development news. The AIG lawyers are suing the US government. What nerve AIG has and what an astounding story! They could get many millions of dollars from the government and we lost all the money from our stocks and most people are in a very difficult situation facing their retirement. Now we are all suffering unbearable stress.

Since today is Saturday, all the conference attendees from Europe already left for home. The breakfast room was almost empty. I brought my food to the table at the window.

A Japanese professor, Koshi Adachi, Director, Center for Tribologically Based Machine Design, joined me. He started a conversation; "My flight will leave this afternoon and arrive in

Japan in the evening". "I could go today but if I do not stay on Saturday, the fare is almost double, so I will leave tomorrow morning," I explained my situation.

"What do you think about the conference?" I started a conversation and continued, "Well, too basic, there is a long way to go to apply to the real world, even though we are already applying nanotechnology now in several fields, such as the medical and pharmaceutical area." "But not in the lubricant area" he interrupted. "Yes. That's true." I realized that he and I were in the same field. "Our company is manufacturing machining lubricants for machines for drilling, tapping, etc., for automotive parts," I continued. "Many companies in Detroit related to the auto industry are having a very tough time." I started to dominate the conversation, "Our lubricant area is macro technology. It is difficult for me to relate with tiny, small particles. Also, this nano research does not connect directly to our real world, at least in the lubricant field."

"That's right. Our young scientists are sticking to an unrealistic area and neglecting the real world." Professor Adachi showed me what his profession is teaching. "But we do need this kind of imagination in the scientific fields which Einstein had," I continued. "That's the reason my research will be bridging two worlds, from macro towards nano." I spoke too energetically, with passion. I forgot the tables in the dining room were almost full. "Yes. By your long experience you can do it and that research will be valuable for young engineers." He praised my experience. That meant I looked old to him.

"Thank you."

He changed the subject. "Any chance to visit Japan?" he asked me. "By the way I will be at the conference 'World congress of tribology' in Kyoto in September," I responded. "Then tour around Japan after the conference." His suggestion was kind. "The schedule is very tight. Before the Kyoto conference, I have to stop in Korea. It is hard to combine three items. A couple of tour companies offer a two week program through Japan including "Yokan" ("traditional Japanese inn"). Yokan is one of the places we have to visit in our lifetime," I continued. "How is the economy in

135

Japan?" "Even though the economy is bad, the government does not cut research projects. The universities are ok," he responded politely. "That's great." This is the first time I heard the organization does not cut the budget. Science and technology are the most important areas for the Japanese people. We almost stood up at the same time. "Have a good trip and see you in September. I am in a conference organizing committee." Professor Adachi told me with a soft smile on his face. "See you then." When we left the breakfast room it was mid-morning.

The fourth day – Sunday unexpected breakfast

Yesterday I made the reservation for the shuttle bus to the airport at 7:00 a.m. through the lobby. To avoid being late I came down to the lobby at 6:30 a.m. for checkout. At the front desk an Indian clerk was at the counter. I paid the room fee and also I was supposed to pay €19 for the shuttle service to the airport.

He was speaking so fast with the Indian accent that it was hard to understand. Of course, he did not understand me either. "Breakfast is ready. If you have time you are welcome to have it." He mentioned this by way of ignoring or showing that he did not understand me about paying the shuttle fare. "I bought a ticket yesterday for the shuttle bus through your counter and I have to pay" I insisted. I spoke clearly and slowly, word by word. Now he understood me and I also pointed out my ticket. "Ya. Ya. Room 308. Yes, your ticket." I handed over my credit card. "No. No. This is nothing to do with the hotel. You have to pay cash." His speech was faster than before like a gunshot.

I gave him coins in order to use them up. First he counted €19 in coin and next he counted the same coins again and then I was €5 short. I hope he did not use a dirty trick because I could not see the numbers on the coins well without a magnifying glass. Since I had about thirty minutes, I left him and I went to the breakfast room. Usually breakfast is 7 – 10 a.m. I thought today may be special. The door was half open. When I went inside there were five Asians at the table, two women and three men.

"Are you Korean?" As usual I started. "Yes. Are you Korean too?" one of the ladies answered. "You are checking out and returning to Korea?" one of the old men continued. "Yes. After the conference I will take the morning flight. Did you come for the conference?" "Yes. We came from the Dajun Nuclear Research Center," again the old, bold man answered. "How many nuclear power plants are there in Korea?" I continued.

"About twenty plants," one of the youngest (about forty years old) men answered. I was surprised that such a small country less than Michigan in area has twenty nuclear plants. Amazing.

I asked a very silly question. "Do you know Mr. Yoon (Kyung Hee) who is a consultant for nuclear plants for Korea through Bobcox-Willcox?" When I asked the question I did not even give them Dr. Yoon's full name. Of course they said no. Dr. Yoon is my engineering alumni in Seoul, Korea and also from the University of Iowa. Several years ago he retired from Bobcox-Willcox. Since his retirement he has been working as a consultant for Korean nuclear power plants. He told us he is busier than before his retirement. I thought he is another lucky man because of his continuous employment. With my stupid question our conversation stopped. The room was so quiet that we could hear the sound of food being chewed.

"Where do you live in Seoul?" one of the ladies asked me. I was so glad that she helped pass over the awkward moment.

"I came from Detroit, Michigan," and I repeated again that I came to Vienna for the conference last week and I added, "It was very cold and windy and on Thursday we had snow." "In Seoul 20 – 25 °C and cherry blossoms at their peak, blooming," another man commented about the weather. "How often do you visit Korea?" the old bold man asked me. "Twice per year," my answer was short. "Since you are coming to Korea, what do you think about Korea? Have there been many changes?" I did not hesitate to give him my answer. "Lots of changes, without a guide it is not easy to find the same places where I went one year ago." They might ask me about political changes but I did not catch the real meaning of their questions in the beginning. Also I do not have any interest in

Korean politics.   Quickly I continued.   "Everything is more expensive than in the USA and lots of wealthy people are in Korea."

"Koreans have lots of money." Again I continued. "When I went to the market with my sister-in-law, the merchant noticed immediately from my appearance that I came from the USA." I was sorry that I had dominated the conversation but I wanted to give them my impressions of Korea.

One lady interrupted. "Yes. Even when we go to the market we dress up by wearing expensive jewelry and show off some good things outside." We think that appearances are most important in our life patterns." *That is very true.* I repeated inside of my mind.

It was five minutes to 7:00 a.m. I told them that my shuttle bus is waiting for me and exchanged "goodbye" and left the breakfast room.

As soon as I came to the lobby a black taxi came for me for the airport. I thought a limousine but maybe Sunday nobody goes to the airport so instead of a limousine, the company sent a taxi. The young driver started to talk about his girlfriend in Toronto working for an auto parts manufacturing company and will be in Toronto for the next year. Maybe he can find a job in Canada.

Exchanging conversation, we arrived at the KLM terminal. I handed over my red ticket. He was surprised that "Not €19. It is €38. It is a taxi. You owe me €19." My surprise was bigger than his. "I bought a ticket for the shuttle bus through the hotel counter, not for a taxi." He called the hotel a couple of times. "You have to deal with the hotel with this situation, not me," I told him firmly and showed him there was no way that he, the taxi driver, should ask me for more money. He spoke to the hotel attendant in German.

I was very dissatisfied with the hotel attendant. He could not communicate with me properly in English and he did not converse well with the limousine company in German either. His speech pattern was too fast and his lack of attention to my needs as a customer cost me extra frustration and brought a loss to the hotel.

AFRICA

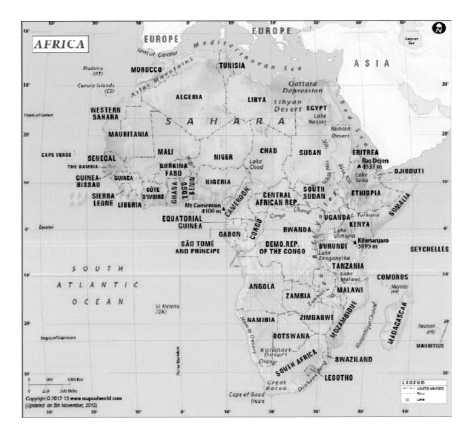

Camel Riding in Egypt

In the middle of November I was standing on the edge of the Sahara Desert a few hundred yards away from the Great Pyramid of Giza. Without a breeze, the warm and dry sun was hitting my head, making me thirsty and even dizzy. I was told there had been no rain in the Giza area for three hundred sixty five days. Even if Egypt doesn't have a rainy season the healthy green vegetation is spread out along the Nile River with one - two miles width on the bank by extremely well planned irrigation. One foot away from the vegetation the vast Sahara Desert is in front of my feet. The small hills, gorges, dunes and mountains of sand are made by the strong wind.

The first thing we did when we arrived at Giza by bus was camel riding before walking around the pyramids. My excitement about riding a camel was beyond imagination. When I was in high school the most desirable thing was horseback riding. Even over the age of seventy, I have not been horse back riding more than once. I thought there was not much difference between the camel and horseback riding.

After the Korean War, we had many demonstrations and parades on the streets with a variety of banners for different occasions. I cannot remember the reasons for the parades but we walked miles and miles in a line under the sizzling sun or chilly rain. At that time, I envied the patrolman or policeman on horseback while controlling the crowd.

I was into a deep fantasy of riding a camel in the desert, creating a post card scene, such as a man on a camel with a wide rim gray hat deep in his face, a cigarette in the left side of his mouth, holding the saddles loosely, moving step by step, to search for an oasis in the pinkish red sky, the small red ball of the sun hung on the horizon of the desert. It is quite an amazing picture of a camel riding against the sunset.

But it was not sunset and not the desert where we were going to ride the camel. It was at rocky ground near the Great Pyramid of Giza about thirty yards from the Sahara Desert. About ten camels lay down on the ground waiting for guests. In Giza three pyramids are lined up. The Great Pyramid was built by Pharaoh Cheops, the next ones were built by Mycerinus and Chepren.

The camel guides were wearing worn out but colorful turbans on their heads, white or light blue tunic clothes and sandals, one assigned to each camel. Their big eyes were wandering, waiting for their guests and their mouths were constantly moving in a chewing motion.

Half of our group decided to go riding and one-half chickened out and just watched the riders. When I looked at my camel, his mean and peculiar character without any personality, I thought that maybe I will be thrown off his back if he plays tricks. My hesitation delayed our group from leaving and in a moment Kwang forced me to ride. No choice. He won all the time over my wishes. I yelled at him, "Kwang, remember I had a difficult time when I went horseback riding in Costa Rica". I did not know how to control the horse at that time. Suddenly, the horse broke into a gallop. Just before I fell off, the horse's owner saved me.

I waited in the saddle on the camel. Actually, it was not a saddle. It was a worn out blanket which had just enough cushion so that I could tolerate the aches in my hips. The camel's head was going up and down and he was rolling his big eyes. Without any warning, he suddenly stood up. "Wow," I screamed.

It was about ten ft. above the ground. There was no good device on the saddle to hold onto the seat. I had to hold on to a two inch by four inch wooden knob on the saddle with both hands. The young camel guide seemed to have lots of tricks which he used to maneuver the camel and fool guests. He frightened people. "OK? OK?" he asked with a big grin. I almost fell down in front of the camel. "Wow. Wow." Kwang also screamed. At that moment Kwang was beside me and he saw my movements on the camel.

"OK?   OK?" the young camel guide questioned again, showing little concern. I just wished he could speak more than "OK. OK." Was this humorous young man starting a game with me? I was holding the wooden knob tightly which was the only thing I could hold. Luckily I did not break the knob. Later I had a big blister on the palm of my hand. "OK?" the young man asked again.

"OK (?). Yeah, I think I am OK." He seemed relieved. My camera was still on my shoulder, so I really was "OK". "OK. OK. No problems?" he probed again and again. He kept asking and demanding my answer. "OK."

"Yeah, but go slowly and hold the camel tightly without running," I continued. I did not know if he understood my long sentence again. "OK. OK." With lower tone, he was relieved that I was all right on the camel's hump and caught on that it did not work with me playing any games.

We rode for about ten yards in the Sahara Desert out of the rocky ground. Now the camel had calmed down and I was "OK" and could look around at the scenery. It was spectacular. To my right was the Sahara Desert, an endless field of sand dunes, and on my left the three pyramids were glistening in the midday sunlight. The sea of brown sand was in front of me with layers and layers of hills and plains. The wind blew the warm sand and it hit my cheeks.

The camel's saddle was getting thinner and it felt like riding on two sheets of paper, or like sitting on a rock, just a single layer of blanket on the camel's hump; no saddle like on the horses in Costa Rica. His steps in the desert into sand are like one foot in a deep hole and the other foot in the air, simulating dancing rock and roll. Getting comfortable and enjoying the ride, now I could handle holding the knob with only one hand and could take pictures of our friends behind me. More relaxed on the hump, I enjoyed taking pictures of the scenery, looking around at the three pyramids and the back side of the sphinx under the azure blue sky.

The camel seemed to settle down too as he sensed the young camel guide's excitement diminish from my screaming. My anxiety

142

was gone about falling down from the camel's hump. I could even feel the nice breeze from the desert. I was going miles, miles and miles on the sand riding on a camel seeking an oasis or shelter and maybe treasure like on the Silk Road thousands of years ago. But it was a very short, twenty minute ride on the sand. The camel guide led us around the Great Pyramid. The Great Pyramid like the other two is made of two million three hundred thousand stones and each stone weighs two - three tons, and its height is one hundred forty six meters. The two others are smaller than the Great One and three other much smaller pyramids, for the king's daughters, are a couple of miles away from this Giza complex.

Around the pyramids, waves of people were admiring the grandeur and the phenomena of the ancient technology, which was used to carry two - three ton stones to the top of the pyramids' one hundred forty six meters height.

The camel guide tried to explain how the pyramids were built and their purpose about five thousand years ago near the Nile River. Instead of catching his words I glued my eyes to the stones and pretended to understand him. "Yes. Yes." and "Um. Um." I responded. He continued to try to explain "King, death and Nile". He tried to explain that many people died in order to build the pyramids, and it is the king's tomb and the stones were carried from the Nile River.

I came to the base of the pyramid. The two to three ton stones were under the base cornerstone or scattered on the ground. Looking at this, my questions could not stop. "How could a human being make this happen five thousand years ago without cranes or any modern equipment?" "How many peoples' lives were sacrificed to build one of the king's pyramids in Egypt? Did the king (pharaoh) have absolute power like God? The people in Egypt worshipped God through the king to get to Heaven?"

Many theories were developed surrounding the pyramids of Egypt. "How, why and the purpose behind the building" are developed by famous historians and archeologists. But my theory is that the Egyptians built the pyramids because they believed in life after death, like Buddhism.

The tour concluded and the camel slowly and smoothly sat down in order to let me out of his saddle easily. I looked at him again. His head was moving right and left again, blinking his large eyes. He did not look mean like when I saw him for the first time.

The camel guide was happy that I did not scream when I got off the camel and asked me for a tip.

Figure 62 Egypt Pyramid

Figure 63 Camel Ride

Figure 64 Camel Ride

Figure 65 Abu Simbel

Tent Hotels In Africa

In order to avoid the sizzling African heat and the rainy season in December, we chose August for our trip to the Serengeti in Tanzania, Africa. Before arriving in the Serengeti, we spent two days in Arusha, Tanzania to gain experience in game plan in Arusha National Park. Our travel group was fifteen people total from New Jersey, New York and other states.

Our early breakfast was a combination of American style bacon and eggs and typical African rice dish with American coffee.

Fifteen people were divided into three land rovers and three guides. Combi was our main guide. Men, women and children were outside on the main street in Arusha. Specifically, the women had water pails or vegetable baskets on their heads and were walking fast without holding it. The basic colors, yellow, red and dark blue dresses of the women with large flower patterns attracted my attention.

After driving less than five miles and passing by a coffee farm, we arrived at the Arusha National Park entrance. The elementary school students were from the bus with uniforms, blue skirts for girls and blue pants for boys with white shirts. A group of local people came to the park and were waiting their turn. After the proper paperwork, our group started to the game plan.

The Land Rover has an open roof that we could stand in to watch the thousands of acres of brown grass spread in the vast land to provide shelter for monkeys, giraffes, zebras, antelope and others.

A couple of zebras were resting peacefully under the shade of an umbrella tree. A flock of antelope were hopping around the giraffes, which were picking berries or leaves from the trees. Two birds were sitting on the giraffe's neck and feeding off the bugs on him and then looked up at the sky for rest. The giraffe started to move, but the poor birds had forgotten how to fly. It was an absolutely beautiful postcard scene with great harmony.

"Kwang, take a picture, take a picture," I shouted without thinking of any consequences. "Be quiet. You almost made the birds fly away," he whispered, while punching my side. A giraffe strolled slowly with his long neck, zebras were jumping around, antelope chased each other with groups. It was a stunning view.

I had only seen wild animals in the cages at the zoo. The mysterious feeling penetrated to my heart about the indescribable phenomenon of the wonders of nature. All the wild animals live together under the blue sky in peace and harmony without fences and without territory.

Combi told us when all of us made exclamations, "This is just an introduction. You will see more wild animals. We will see lions, cheetah, hyenas and leopards in the Serengeti National Park." Everybody mouthed "oh, oh" in chorus.

After a picnic lunch in the park, we came back to the hotel. Combi gave us a briefing for tomorrow's Serengeti trip, and he warned us that there would be three - four hours rough ride from Arusha.

The next morning we again divided into three groups. The pleasant sunlight was pouring on our faces and the clear blue sky was following us. Everybody was in a good mood, with great expectations and we exchanged joyful greetings, "Good morning" and "Good morning."

"We might see lions today," a lady from New Jersey spoke with a high-pitched voice.

"I hope so," was added by Combi, whose voice did not show assurance that we would see the lions. Maybe he did not want to give us false expectations.

About three to four miles of smooth riding was ended and we were on a dirt road between the tall prairie grass on both sides. The height of the grass was taller than my height. It was the perfect place to make shelter for the animals. The brown waves were dancing waltzes along with the wind. It was a golden horizon. By the travel agent's guidebook's instructions we all wore light brown clothes to match the color of the grass to avoid exciting the animals with primary colors, red, blue and yellow.

The bumpy road made us jump from the seats to the ceiling and our backs were rubbing against the seats. It was a long, dangerous ride. Combi broke the silence to cheer us up. "This is the African massage. This is the only place in the world this is offered, so please enjoy it. It is free of charge for special guests." Combi was aware of the serious risk of back injuries, but there was nothing he could do. In the car the seat belts were missing or they were hard to buckle up because they were rusty, and so we held tight to the head rest in front of us.

The oncoming cars created clouds of sand dust when they passed us. Even covering my mouth with a scarf did not prevent the sand from getting in my nose and mouth. Also, our guide's vision was hampered because of driving through the sand blanket. "Kwang, cover your camera with a plastic bag. The camera lens is covered with sand," I warned him.

The African massage and fighting the dust were unexpected difficulties we had to adapt to. A lady from New Jersey was complaining, "Instead of riding in a car, we could fly this long distance. This is ridiculous … this shower of dust." Before her words were finished, Combi remarked, "This is a much better choice. In summertime in Africa it is the rainy season and the road is flooded and the car gets stuck in the mud and the worst thing is the mosquitoes. Last summer the car was stuck in the mud and everybody had to get out and push the car." He emphasized with an uneasy voice this is the best choice for this season and there is no other way.

"Just a couple of hours more and we will arrive at our hotel soon." Everybody was quiet because we were scared to open our mouths for fear that the sand would rush in.

We finally arrived near the Serengeti National Park and saw elephants with their babies, and at a short distance we could see a couple of lions were in the bush looking at us.

Everybody forgot the difficulties we had on the way and we all stood up and shouted "lions, lions". Immediately Combi warned us, "Be quiet. You never know about the behavior of wild animals. Let's not get them excited."

Finally we arrived at our tent hotel and dusted the sand off, from head to toes. When I touched my face, it was as rough as sandpaper. Seven tents were for our group and one tent was for our guide and a big tent was the dining hall. These tents were nothing like I dreamed about which was similar to the movie "Out of Africa." The dark green color was reminiscent of military camp. I was getting dizzy just thinking about spending four nights here. Inside the tent there were two simple camp beds approximately one foot off the ground covered with a layer of foam over plywood and two windows on the sides with mosquito mesh and the tent's height was enough that I could stand in the middle. We put our luggage on our beds and went out for the briefing. Combi started to mention the rules for staying in the tent.

"The tent hotel is more expensive than the regular hotel," Kwang tried to comfort me and to explain that he did his best to give me a new and adventurous experience in Africa.

"I don't care about the price, but I would rather sleep in a regular bed in a hotel."

"Hey, calm down. Your voice is so loud that they will hear your ugly complaining in the next tent. Nobody else is complaining. You are the only one." His voice was full of anger. "How about ants? Ants may climb into the bed," I spoke through my tears.

The cold war lasted for a long time between Kwang and I. I had tried to calm my anger and my pounding heart. In the next split second I thought, let's get the best out of these unusual circumstances.

What can I get from this? I do not know I spoke to myself.

We would spend four nights here for the Serengeti game plan," Combi continued, "Keep absolutely every window and door in the tent closed against the mosquitoes and the animals at night. Also, put everything inside the tent, including your shoes."

"What does that mean, animals?" questioned the man from New York.

"As you can see, antelope, elephants, zebras and giraffes make their home here and we have to share with them," Combi politely answered the question.

"What about other animals, lions and cheetahs?"

"Quite possible," Combi's answer was very short, trying to escape from unexpected questions from the group, and he continued, "Through the night at the front of the tent a lantern will hang with a light to keep the animals away."

"If the light goes out, what should we do?" a lady from New Jersey questioned with concern.

"Then you are in big trouble. You may have a lion as a guest." Combi's joke made the lady frozen. "Do not worry. In case of danger, blow the whistle." We (guides and crew) are only fifteen feet away from you." Then Combi gave whistles to each person and continued to explain about the bathroom and shower facility. The bathroom is outside attached to the main tent with one long bar and there was space between the bathroom and the tent. Combi explained the bathroom business very humorously. "After you have business in the bathroom, you have to cover it with dirt which is in the small bucket with a small shovel.

"The shower you have to manage with five gallons of water. Five gallons is more than enough for a shower. We will provide the warm water."

151

Combi was going to continue but we all screamed. "Five gallons? Five gallons? It is impossible to have a shower with only five gallons of water."

"First turn the valve slowly, wet your hair and body using as small an amount of water as possible, and then close the valve. Next step, use soap and shampoo, then rinse with the remaining water." "Five gallons is enough for your showers," Combi again assured us about the quantity of water.

"A long time ago a lady did not pay attention to my instructions and she used up the entire amount of her water wetting her body. She was covered with soap and shampoo and blew the whistle for more water in distress." All the crew members and antelope rushed to the lady covered with shampoo." Before Combi finished his last sentence everybody burst into laughter wondering if this was a true story or made up.

We will check the lantern lights often during the night. As long as the light is on at the front of the tent, we will not expect any incidents," Combi continued, "You will experience several different noises during the night, wind, lions groaning, elephant steps, or giraffes going through the trees. But nothing has happened for the last several years."

We were all relieved by the news that nothing had happened for the last several years, but we still all had serious concerns that first night in the tent in the wild African prairie.

The rest of the afternoon we explored for more wild animals, cheetahs, hyenas, and, of course, more lions. Two lions with two cubs took a nap on top of the huge flat rocks.

One hundred yards away a lonely cheetah was walking slowly, looking for meat for his dinner. "Look at this. Look at this," Combi screamed. He forgot that he should not scream in the game plan. "That side. Over there."

"Where? Where?" we all responded together. We tried to spot the object but could not see it.

"About fifty yards away, between the small trees, he is running," Combi directed us to the spot.

"Yes. Yes. There," Kwang and a gentleman from New York confirmed the object with their binoculars. I took out my small binoculars and looked at the scene. What a spectacular scene! A hyena was chasing a zebra who was behind his flock. I did not know if he was sick or just a baby, but I knew this ... the hyena would put him on his dinner table.

We came back to our tent hotel and, yes, faxes from Chrysan in Michigan were waiting for us with several items of news. After dinner we sat around the campfire with coffee under the stars. I have never seen so many bright stars in the sky and they were so low we could almost pluck them from the sky. In a Chinese poem, the scholars studied under the light from the stars and the moon. It could be true.

Combi started a serious discussion on Tanzanian politics, such as circumcision for girls and financial aid from different organizations. The aid does not reach the people who really need it and even if it does reach them, it is only in tiny portions. We all admired his concern about Tanzania and wanted to help him in some way.

The lantern with a bright light hung in front of our tent, dancing in the rhythm of the wind. The night in Africa was getting cold and it was time for sleep. Combi gave flashlights to each person and assured us that nothing would happen and said to make sure to "Put the flashlight and whistle near your pillow."

We exchanged "good night" with misgivings that I could not verbalize. With uncertainty about spending the night in the tent, we laid down. I could not sleep. I pushed down my eyelids with my left hand and with my right one I touched the flashlight and whistle for reassurance in case of unexpected things. "Kwang, are you sleeping?"

"No, I cannot." "Everything will be ok," with a weak voice Kwang comforted me.

"Yeah, sure, it will be fine."

With the flapping noise of the tent, the whistling sound of the tree branches and my imagination of the growling noise of lions and footsteps of elephants, I could not sleep. The more I tried to sleep, the more I stayed awake with vivid pictures of a cloud of sand blocking the driver's vision, the manes and the roaring of the lions, a hyena chasing a zebra and a parade of dik-diks and one elephant had five legs. I could not sleep and I touched the flashlight and whistle again.

Finally, in spite of Kwang's snoring, the flapping noise of the tent and the whistling sound of the branches, I had fallen asleep. With the dawn I woke up and found I still had the whistle in my left hand and the flashlight in my right hand. Both hands were sweating profusely.

With Combi's wake up call at each tent with "good morning," we all came out of our tents. The warm water was waiting for us in the basin for washing our face and hands and the lanterns still showed us their lights.

We exchanged our last night experiences of noises around the tents "our hotels", at the breakfast table. Combi mentioned that in our campground he assumed that two lions came by. Everybody rolled their eyes in fear and surprise. "How do you know?"

Combi explained that during the night he heard the lions growling and he saw the footprints. "After breakfast I will show you the lion's footprints."

Everybody was silent and seemed to be in deep meditation thinking about the fact that we slept in the wild animal kingdom and felt a mixture of thrill and fear for three more nights.

Figure 66 Serengeti Tent with Shower Bucket

Figure 67 Serengeti Dining Room

Figure 68 Animals around Tents

Figure 69 Animals around Camp Site

Figure 70 Animals around Tents

Figure 71 Animals around Camp

157

Figure 72 Monkey with Baby

Figure 73 Lion

Climbing Mt. Kilimanjaro

Climbing Mt. Kilimanjaro was not on our list of fifty places to visit in our lifetime. But during our vacations at various famous tourist attractions we had heard that climbing Mt. Kilimanjaro is exciting, challenging and rewarding. In November 2007 our friend, Jerry from General Motors, who was about sixty years old, told us that he climbed Mt. Kilimanjaro twice, using different routes. This increased our interest in climbing to Kibo on Kilimanjaro and we had a meeting with Jerry who gave us information and advice.

In February or March 2008 we decided to go ahead and took the greatest risk of our lives. Subsequently Kwang started collecting more information from different sources and information about travel agents. I did not know there were so many different programs for climbing Mt. Kilimanjaro, five - six days, six - seven days and ten days, adding at least one to one and one-half days for descending.

We chose Tusker Kilimanjaro Travel Group for the eight days ascending program. It was quite pricey, but for our age, this was the best way for success in reaching the summit.

Kwang was looking at programs for reaching the summit on January 1, 2009 but the airfare was about $4,000 during the Christmas and New Year's holidays, almost double the normal fare. We chose departure on December 10 and a return on December 24, 2008. Then we contracted the eight day ascending and one and one-half day descending program with Tusker in the middle of July 2008.

The reason we chose Tusker was because the guides were well trained for medical emergencies and they carried two oxygen tanks with their emergency equipment. Also, Tusker did not limit the ages of climbers, but we had to submit detailed medical information.

In July 2008 Kwang started preparations for our trip. First, we had all the travel gear and equipment but we could not use most of it. We had to prepare new gear and layers of lightweight clothing. The clothes had to be silk or wool underwear, which are quick drying and much lighter than cotton when wet. Absolutely no cotton clothes allowed. Boots were to be waterproof, gaiters, gloves. Clothes ranged from the tropical rain forest to Arctic weather. Some gear had to be special ordered, and some we bought at local sporting goods stores.

The down sleeping bag weighed about two pounds. and can be comfortable up to −5 °F. Not only did we have to prepare our gear and equipment, but our physical condition had to be perfect. We pushed ourselves to exercise with fifteen pounds weights to strengthen our backs, and walked at least one hour daily for six months. The reason for the fifteen pounds weights is that we would be carrying about four liters of water and rain gear and personal necessities in our daypacks. Tusker recommended drinking at least four liters of water per day to prevent dehydration.

Kwang was reading more information on Kilimanjaro's history, mortality rates, etc. and the success rates for reaching the summit. He discovered on the Internet that there was a fifty percent success rate and about thirty people died per year (later the guide told us that about three people die annually). Maybe the statistics included porters.

Three months before the trip we checked all our gear and started the physical exercise, but for me the timing was not right. I could not exercise as much as I wanted. Two months before leaving we checked the gear again and broke in our new boots. Then, one month before departure we checked the equipment again, and I started to exercise about forty minutes daily and included walking backwards for twenty minute and forwards for twenty minutes outside in our office parking lot. Kwang stopped drinking any alcohol except at the family reunion which was our family vacation at Thanksgiving in Cancun, Mexico.

Two weeks before our journey our new backpacks with two liter water pouches arrived. A connected hose would allow us to drink water while walking.

One week before we left we started packing snack bars, Baby Ruths, chocolate, almond crunch and Gatorade powder packets to give us energy.

Two days before we left we did our final packing and put one set of gear in our daypack. In case our check-in luggage did not arrive on time, we could still climb to the summit using the clothes in our daypack.

About two weeks before going to Mt. Kilimanjaro, NBC (Today) correspondent Ann Curry went to Kilimanjaro without success. Ann Curry led five crew members from NBC and one hundred supporting team members to study ecological changes in the Mt. Kilimanjaro area. They retreated at sixteen thousand feet because of the cold and high altitude sickness.

Honestly, before this news, I was excited about our plans to reach the Kibo summit on Kilimanjaro, but now my excitement was completely gone and was replaced by fear and nervousness.

Friends, church members and our children said, "Do not take risks and come back safely. If you do not reach the summit, it is enough that you were at the foot of Mt. Kilimanjaro." My daughter said, "Mom, I don't want to see your picture at the summit, just come back safely." These comments generated more scary thoughts in my mind. With a shaky voice I told Kwang, "Let's not take risks."

We are going to take the specially made Chrysan banner to the top of "Kibo". What would happen to the "Chrysan Banner" if we do not make it?

On December 10, 2008 Kwang and I left the office at 1:30 p.m. All our employees lined up to wish us good luck on our trip, and I could see the concern in their eyes. Our flight left for Amsterdam at 5:45 p.m.

On December 11, 2008 we arrived at Kilimanjaro airport around 7:30 p.m. The flying time from Detroit to Amsterdam was seven and one-half hours and from Amsterdam to Kilimanjaro

Airport was eight and one-half hours. The Tusker jeep met us at the airport. Kwang and I, Predeep from Boston, who was one of our five members, transferred us to the Keys Hotel in Moishi, Tanzania about a one hour drive from the airport. The hotel room was very basic, two twin beds, shower and running water in the bathroom and a fan on the wall. Two members of our group from Australia had not arrived yet.

On <u>December 12, 2008</u> there was an 11:00 a.m. briefing on climbing. Kombe, our main guide, and Frank, the assistant guide, who was very short even though his parents are Masai, came for a briefing for the ten days schedule, "Shoulds and Should nots," items, and activities for climbing.

After the briefing Kombe checked all our gear that we spread out on the bed. He told us what we absolutely needed to take and we left the remaining gear and material at the hotel for ten days. In the morning, Karen and Simon from Australia joined us, so our group totaled five members.

On <u>December 13, 2008</u> the last night shower was the last shower for ten days. I could not imagine how I would survive for ten days without feeling clean.

At 10:00 a.m. the ascending route was the Lemosho route. After a three and one-half hour drive to the park entrance from the hotel, we registered at the gate for entrance to the park. Another forty minute drive through potato farms, we arrived at the last spot the car could enter. During the drive, our truck was stuck in the mud a couple of times but with skilled driving experience, we managed to get out of the mud. We stopped for a snack lunch at the edge of the Rain Forest and started to ascend to Forest Camp (nine thousand one hundred sixty three feet) where we spent the first night in the tent.

Ann Curry and our friend Jerry both mentioned a terrible experience with pouring rain in the Rain Forest. Kilimanjaro weather changes from minute to minute and Kombe strongly recommended that we carry rain gear in our daypack all the time, even on sunny days.

162

We were lucky to have had sunny skies, but often clouds passed by, like huge waves. In the whole ten days we never experienced rain. After about a six-hour walk we arrived at Forest Camp. First, we ate dinner in the tent. Tusker set up our two people tents along with a big tent as a dining area, and a private toilet for Tusker members instead of natural one. Our group consisted of five climbers, two guides and twenty-six porters, including a cook. Dinner was fried fish, potatoes and vegetables and soup. The first dinner was excellent. Kwang and I both ate good portions.

Tusker strongly recommended keeping in mind the following words "SWAT":

S – sugar – need sugar as a supplement for energy
W – water – drink plenty of water
A – always keep yourselves clean and dry
T – temperature – be prepared for the cold

Tusker always provided sanitary water in front of the dining tent before meals. I think it was bleached water. During dinner Kombe and Frank asked us about any concerns we had, like headaches, diarrhea, nausea, etc., or anything and then checked our oxygen level and pulse and listened to the lung capacity and cleanness. So far everyone was healthy, which heightened the groups' excitement and lightened our mood. We were looking forward to climbing again tomorrow.

Surprisingly, Kwang and I got new nicknames from the guides and porters: Bee-Bee (Grandma) for me and Baboo (Grandpa) for Kwang. We liked it.

Tomorrow morning wake up time was at 6:30 a.m., so we went to our tent around 8:30 p.m. I could see the moonlight through the tent. It was not a full moon but I could see the dim light. I tried to get a sound sleep, because tomorrow would be a long walk.

On December 14, 2008, our sleeping bag was very comfortable. In Kilimanjaro, the weather in the daytime is hot summer and we needed suntan lotion and the evenings were a bitter

Arctic cold. Last night I slept very comfortably in the sleeping bag inside the tent.

During breakfast we had a medical check. In the morning Kombe and Frank checked not only our oxygen level and pulse, but also our lungs to make sure they were clear and that we were taking Malarone and Diamox. Also, Frank was keeping thorough medical records.

Today on the way to Shira Camp One (eleven thousand five hundred feet) we would eat a hot lunch at the Scott Fisher Camp. I could not believe we could have hot food for dinner and breakfast in the tent during our trip, and even lunch was a hot meal. This luxury was unexpected.

In the rain forest, we used the tree's shadows to avoid direct sunlight and the unknown flowers with primitive colors. Kombe had tight schedules for leading us on our route, and he did not allow me more time to take pictures. I wish I had more Kodak moments.

"Bee-Bee, we have gorillas in this rain forest, but we cannot go."

"Why not? Let's see them," was my request.

"No. They are living in a certain area that's not near here". He paused for a moment, then continued, "Bee-Bee and Baboo, be careful. You never know, they may come out in this area". We were quiet.

About one and one-half hours trekking after the Rain Forest, we came to a heather zone with lots of heather trees three to five feet high shrub like trees surrounded by big rocks and we had to maneuver through these rocks. With the heather trees, after pressing them together, they make beautiful jewelry. I bought a pendant.

As the days went on, my backpack became heavier and heavier. Ten – fifteen pounds loaded in my bag was almost too much for me to handle.

In the next instant, one minute there was sun, the next, the sky darkened with an influx of clouds and barraged by winds. When we arrived at the Scott Fisher Camp a hot lunch with chicken was waiting for us. Even though we walked "pole, pole," (This means slowly, slowly in Swahili), we needed lots of energy. I was beginning to lose my appetite, Kwang too.

To support our energy, Kwang and I started to drink cocoa in the morning in a four ounce cup, three teaspoons cocoa, two teaspoons milk (dry) and three teaspoons of sugar and we washed our food down with this cocoa drink. Karen, Simon and Predeep had very good appetites. Simon might eat five times and Karen maybe three times our portions. They were young with good appetites. It was hard for us to keep up with their pace with the adjustment in altitude, they adjusted to the "pole, pole" pace. It was easier than the Patagonia trip. In many places, I had to use my two hands and two legs for crawling on the rocks. Luckily this time I used only two legs. The order of the line was Kombe in the front and then me, Kwang and Predeep and the two Australians, Frank (the assistant guide) and Emmanuel, who was carrying medical equipment, including the oxygen tanks.

After lunch, Predeep declared he could not continue to climb any more. He was just fifty two years old. He was vomiting. Maybe psychologically he was scared to climb and that's why he vomited. His pulse and oxygen level were normal.

Kombe and Frank tried to convince him his condition was perfect to continue. Predeep decided it was not worth risking his life.

Kombe and Frank agreed to evacuate him down. Kombe asked him if he could walk down and Predeep said "No" in a strong voice.

He needed a stretcher and medical attention.

From Emmanuel's emergency yellow bag, he pulled out a stretcher, a sleeping bag and an oxygen tank. Predeep was in a sleeping bag and six porters rushed him down to a spot where it would be possible for a car to pick him up and take him to a doctor for medical care.

On December 15, so far Kwang and I were managing our climbing. Whenever we rested, we supplemented our diet with a Baby Ruth as an energy bar. I had brought enough that I could share with the porters. Kombe noticed that my backpack was very heavy for my weight and he assigned Niki, one of the porters, to carry my daypack allowing me to walk with two sticks. It was a very wise decision, making it much easier for me to make a continuous ascent with less of a struggle.

Kwang lost more of his appetite. It was becoming harder for him to manage himself and I gave him a cocoa drink with lots of sugar. I had never consumed such large amounts of cocoa and brown sugar in my life. As I previously mentioned, the daytime weather at Kilimanjaro is summer and the nighttime weather is freezing Arctic cold sleeping in the tent. In the tent we had two long wool underwear sets and the same at the top and a windbreaker. We slept that way in the sleeping bag with two sets of socks and each foot was encased in a thick wool sweater. Kwang even wore gloves and, of course, we wore wool ski hats. It was difficult to go to the bathroom wearing this many layers to protect us against the frostbite.

When we came out from the tent we saw the white frost covering the ground and the roofs of tents. "Wow. It is cold," Kombe told us with his hands in his pockets. The mist from the cold was coming from everyone's mouth.

Kombe and Frank tested our physical condition again more carefully since Predeep retreated last night.

"Bee-Bee and Baboo, everything is okay, good shape," Frank declared on our condition.

On December 16, the bright sunshine quickly melted the frost. Now we are at thirteen thousand six hundred five feet high. Today's destination was the Lava Tower, fifteen thousand feet altitude.

Kilimanjaro is divided into five zones: Rain Forest, Heather zone, Heather and Moor zone, Alpine Desert and Summit. Now we passed the Heather and Moor zone and we were in the Alpine Desert.

The Alpine Desert consists of big and small rocks. Only three varieties of plants grow here. The gray and blackish volcanic rocks, which look like pine trees, were all over the mountain.

As we kept moving I noticed my silk gloves were getting holes because of holding the stick poles too tightly, and my silk underwear was running like pantyhose.

Still we were climbing with 'pole, pole' pace, but we had to rest more frequently. We still had a plentiful supply of Baby Ruth and energy and almond bars.

In the Heather and Moor Zone nothing was beautiful, though occasionally the white clouds passed under our feet.

As we moved into the Lava Tower, it was getting colder at night. An ice ring formed around the water in our cups even inside the tent. If you looked at the Kibo top, it was just in front of us from our tent. It seemed close but we still had a long way to go. I think Ann Curry climbed about one thousand feet more than the Lava Tower and retreated. The Lava Tower is at fifteen thousand feet and it only has a couple of big rocks with a small creek running behind it. Kwang lost more and more of his appetite. So far I was fine.

On December 17, our destination was the Baranco Camp, about thirteen thousand feet, so we actually descended two thousand feet from the Lava Tower. It was quite challenging.

We had to cross the Baranco wall. It is a tall and huge mountain-like rock wall. The size is much smaller than one piece of rock, like "Ayers" in Australia, but this rock was like a small rocky mountain. We did not climb the rock wall but went around the wall by climbing adjacent rocky areas. Kombe, Frank and the porters pulled me up to the next position on the rocks. Luckily, I do not weigh two hundred pounds Kombe pulled me, and Frank and the porters helped by pushing me.

Among these rocks we could see small mice when we had a break. My stomach was getting uncomfortable and it seemed as though I might have diarrhea. So far I did not have nausea, headaches or swelling fingers, but all day long my stomach was uncomfortable.

The Tusker rule is that we have to tell every symptom that we have and they strongly discourage us from using our own pills, except Malarone or Diamox. I had Imodium from home at night, because I could not wait for next morning. I told Kombe at lunchtime I had Imodium last night. Boy oh boy! He was not happy at all about this matter, because the pill was not from Tuskers. Kombe gave me two tablets. It stops diarrhea from becoming soft bowel movements.

For six days we spent the night in the tent without a shower. We only changed our underwear and socks once and wore the same clothes every day, but we did not feel the itching or smell because of the dry and cold weather.

On December 18, today our destination is the Karanga Camp (thirteen thousand eight hundred feet), almost horizontal from the Baranco Camp. Kwang and I both lost our appetites and the greasy fried chicken dishes made us worse. The food was generally excellent, I just could not eat it.

Usually we started with very nice sunny days in the morning, but as we started climbing we had sunshine one minute and the next minute massive clouds were hitting us with strong winds. We took off layers of clothes one minute and put them on again in another minute. At night it was not as cold at the Karanga Camp as it was at the Lava Tower because of the two thousand foot difference in altitude.

On December 19, today from the Karanga Camp to Barafu Camp (fifteen thousand feet) which is the base camp to the summit. We were still in the Alpine Desert. This time we walked on slate. I could not understand where the slate came from. Some slate was as thin as paper. I thought the best application of it was for roofs.

At the Barafu Camp the porters divided into two groups. One group was going with four climbers (us) to the Crater Camp and the other group stayed in Barafu for two nights.

Our luggage was divided too. We were encouraged to carry only our warmest clothes and sleeping bags, which were absolutely necessary for very cold weather at the Crater Camp (eighteen thousand seven hundred feet) and Kombe and Frank asked us very critical questions, such as did we have confidence that we could climb to the summit. Of course, the Australian young couple did not have any problem, but Kombe and Frank were not one hundred percent sure about Kwang and me.

Kwang lost more appetite and the worst thing was he does not eat chicken dishes. The only energy sources for him were the cocoa drink in the morning and energy bars. I was still fine. Kombe asked Kwang, "Baboo, do you think you can make it?" and he continued, "How about Bee-Bee?" I responded quickly, even though I had some reservations, "Yes. Sure". Then Kombe continued the questions, "If Baboo cannot make it, Bee-Bee can go alone and Baboo can stay here and vice-versa". With little hesitation Kwang and I said, "Yes".
.
December 20 was the most challenging day as we ascended almost four thousand foot climb from fifteen thousand to nineteen thousand three hundred forty feet to summit "Uhuru" in Kibo and we had to sleep in the cold, cold Arctic weather with a glacier on the next side.

I found a very useful trick, which is while I was walking I just looked at the footsteps of the person ahead of me (Kombe). I did not look at the top of the mountain which is far away. If you look at the top of the mountain and the next mountain, you might be choked from the pressure of difficulties. As usual, Kombe, Bee-Bee (Me), Baboo (Kwang) and the two Australians, Frank and Emmanuel, and Niki were in the line.

Today we started early at 5:00 a.m. woke up and were supposed to start ascending at 6:00 a.m. but started at 6:30 a.m. and continuously ascending, ascending, even under the sun, strong winds buffeted us on our cheeks like cold knives.

Kwang and I struggled more than before from short breath and thirst and asked for frequent rests. A couple of days Niki was carrying my daypack and this morning Frank was carrying Kwang's daypack. Kwang wouldn't give up carrying his signature heavy Cannon camera, but now he was struggling with the heavy camera. Emmanuel took it and Kombe had Kwang's small digital camera and took pictures occasionally.

Around 2:30 p.m. we finally arrived at the "Stellar Point", one of the highest points on Kibo on Kilimanjaro, next to Uhuru Peak point. We hugged each other in relief and excitement at our success and climbed for about another hour to reach "Uhuru" the high point at Kibo on Kilimanjaro.

Bright sunshine was with us and on the left and right we could see a wall of glacier. It was beautiful, shining under the sun like a silver mountain among thousands of green mountains spread under my feet and above the mountains white clouds were peacefully floating.

Finally, It was 3:30 p.m. and we were at Uhuru. Kombe continuously took our pictures, including the glaciers.

We stayed at the top for about twenty minutes. There were no clouds at the glacier. We could see the crater, glacier and mountains around Kibo. Group and individual pictures were taken using the "Chrysan" and "ENEOS" Banners. Then we came down to the Crater Camp inside of the crater, which was surrounded by a glacier wall. We slid down to the Crater Camp from Uhuru by skiing among the coarse sand and small gravel. We all felt a huge sense of achievement and excitement, and we were in a celebration mood and proud of ourselves climbing up "Uhuru" at our age. Kwang was seventy four and I was seventy two years old.

The altitude was nineteen thousand three hundred forty feet This was the most challenging experience I ever had, Kwang too, at "Uhuru".

With tremendous joy I told Kwang, "Let's try to climb the base camp of the Himalayas," and continued, "I heard almost everybody makes it".

"Actually, the height of the base camp is almost the same height of Uhuru," Kwang showed his interest in another adventure.

However, Kwang started to vomit and I had a slight headache. Frank gave me two small pills and he gave Kwang a small dose of oxygen and two pills and let him sleep. The altitude was nineteen thousand three hundred forty feet.

At the Crater Camp, our tents were already up and flopping in the strong wind which almost blew me away. The sun was getting ready to hide on the peak of Uhuru. It was a tremendous joy and a once in a lifetime achievement, even if our tents were in the middle of nowhere, surrounded by glaciers, for us it was an absolutely stunning view.

Kombe and Frank never skipped the physical examinations. They were glad we made it without giving them big trouble. I forgot what we had for dinner but it should be delicious.

Kombe suggested we have three layers of under wear and top for a total of four layers for the night in the tent and they provided us one liter each of hot water bottles for our sleeping bags. With many layers and hot water bottle I slept warm but the water in the cup in the tent was frozen.

The Crater Camp's height is eighteen thousand seven hundred feet and it was the coldest night that we had. The wind and the noise of the wind buffeted the tent and it felt as though the wind was blowing our tent away.

The water supply in the Crater Camp comes from glaciers, melted and filtered and boiled for us. This took extra time.

On December 21, descending around the crater and today's plan is at the Barafu Camp to have a hot lunch and take off some layers of clothes and put it into a tote bag which we left at Barafu Camp. We slept at the Millennium Camp (thirteen thousand feet) and stopped using Diamox. The porters, Karen and Simon were descending by jumping. They were way ahead of us. My appetite was getting a little better and I had four scoops of vegetable soup and rice with a mushroom sauce. Millennium Camp is in the Heather and Moor zone. It was much warmer than the Crater Camp.

On December 22, in the morning, there was white frost on the campground. With a heavy windbreaker and two layers of clothes as we descended we took off layer by layer, passing the Heather and Moor zone and the Rain Forest. We were very lucky that we did not have any rain. Beautiful sunshine flowed over us. Sunlight peeked through the leaves in the Rain Forest. Three toes on each foot were hurting, and my right knee (arthritis) bothered me and I could not jump down any more. Kombe, Karen, Simon and one porter left us for the destination today.

I was struggling to descend. Frank suggested that Emmanuel give me a ride on his shoulders, instead of carrying his medical equipment. For a moment I hesitated, but the group could not wait for my slow walk. I rode on his shoulders holding his hands. He jumped down like a kangaroo to the meeting place resting only twice. Maybe my weight was less than his equipment.

Karen, Simon, Kombe and the porter had just finished lunch when Emmanuel and I arrived. In ten minutes the Tusker truck arrived, and in about fifteen minutes, Kwang, Frank and Niki and Dayle joined us. After about one hour drive, we arrived at the Keys Hotel around 2:30 p.m. on December 22, 2008.

Our journey was over, climbing under the sun, above the clouds, braving strong winds with waves of clouds, five zones of land of Kilimanjaro. It was not easy to conquer this at my age.

After a hot shower at 4:00 p.m., we five members sat together, including Predeep, reviewing the Tusker service and wanting to hear feedback. They gave us a certification for climbing Mt. Kilimanjaro. It felt great.

Figure 74 Mt. Kilimanjaro

Figure 75 Barranco Camp and Walls

Figure 76 Barranco Camp and Walls

Figure 77 At the Uhuru Peak

Figure 78 Ice Field inside Uhuru Crater

Figure 79 **Descending from Summit**

175

Figure 80 Descending

Figure 81 Celebrating Successful Summiting

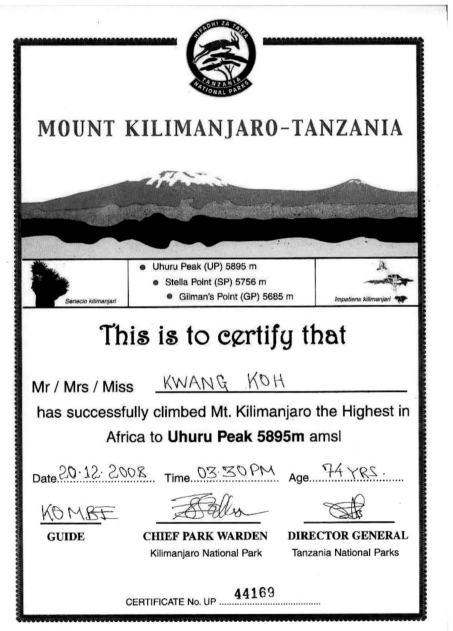

Figure 82 Certificate of Successful Summiting

177

Figure 83 Cerebration after Descending

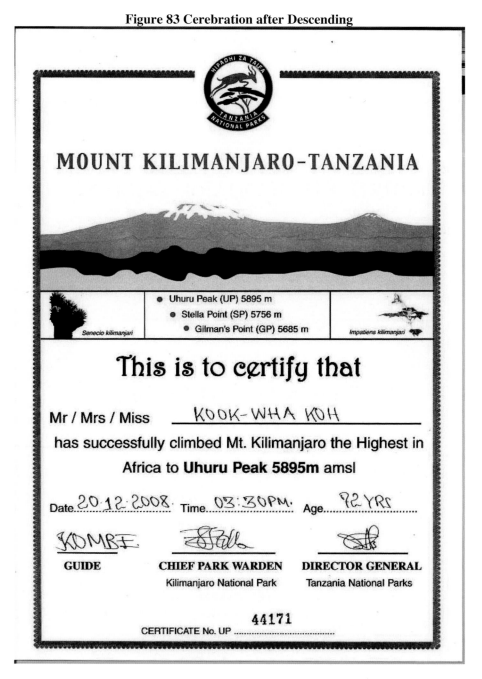

Figure 82 Certificate for summiting Mt. Kilimanjaro

Controversial Topics in Africa

In the middle of December 2011, to avoid the cold and snowy winter in Detroit, we had a chance to go on safari in Botswana, Zambia and Zimbabwe. We enjoyed the sizzling heat in the daytime and nice cool breezes in the evening in Southern Africa. December in Africa is damp with high humidity. The rainy season, with 20 – 30 minutes rain showers per day, was the typical summer weather.

Our group had thirteen people from the USA and Tenash was our travel guide from Zimbabwe. He introduced himself, thirty two years old and he and his wife have a little girl about one year old. He was not only punctual, but also gave us detailed and thorough information on the subjects.

The first National Park for our safari was Chobe National Park in Botswana. After we unloaded our luggage at the tent lodge in the Park which has a private shower and running water facility in each room and, to my surprise, there was a mosquito net attached around the bed. We gathered at the main lobby for a briefing and had welcoming drinks. The lobby had rotating ceiling fans with very slow speed and no walls around the buildings. It was open toward the huge national park, but at the center of the lobby there were arm chairs and dark brown sofas made of cloth, and on the tea table several magazines about Africa and books on African flowers, animals and birds were scattered.

Thirteen people in our group acted like a huge family or one military unit for eighteen days on a safari camp.

Tenash asked us straightforwardly to each person, "What we are expecting or want to see on this trip." Almost all of us said, "We want to see leopards, cheetahs and rhinos." Pat from Oklahoma mentioned, "I want to see baby elephants". Tenash responded without any hesitation, "I cannot promise all, but we will try our best, let's see".

Then it was my turn. "Last time we were on safari in Serengeti in Tanzania we did not see any leopards, so I would like to see them, like the other people mentioned, leopards, rhinos and cheetahs," and continued, "Wait a minute, I would like to add one more thing, the spectacular Victoria Falls, because I saw other famous falls: Niagara Falls, Angel Falls and Iguazu Falls," and added, "To see Victoria Falls is my highlight". Kwang nudged me, "You are saying too much. Please, can you stop?"

Twice per day we did game viewing. We woke up at 5:30 a.m. and had a quick continental breakfast. From 6:00 a.m. to 10:30-11:00 a.m., we were driving through the park to watch the animals. When we left Detroit at almost 8:00 a.m., it was still dark, but in Chobe National Park (in Africa) 5:00 a.m., it was dawn. By 5:30 a.m., it was bright morning and at 7:00 p.m. it was getting dark with a beautiful sunset. In Detroit it became dark at 5:00 p.m.

Thirteen people were divided into two groups in the four wheel truck which had only a roof and seats to drive through the park. Tanesh emphasized, "Please, see through the wood for looking for animals, do not look at the wood." We all burst into laughter and repeated "through the wood, not at the wood."

We spent a couple of days at Chobe National Park, and saw lions, wild dogs, hippos, elephants and impalas and unknown birds everywhere.

We had siesta time between 1:00-3:30 p.m., before heading for game viewing again in the afternoon. We discussed several topics over tea, such as AIDS and its progress. The good news is the number of AIDS patients is decreasing from twenty five percent to seventeen percent and they are living longer than before with preventive medicine and educational programs. Packages of condoms were everywhere, in the airport lobby and in public restrooms (women or men, it does not matter) with signs "free, take it". The education about AIDS starts even in elementary school children. The awareness and concerns of AIDS problems in Africa are leveled out by the immense financial aid and project of medical devices from around the world. We just had a brief discussion.

The next interesting topic was democracy in Africa, especially in Zimbabwe. Tenash, our guide from Zimbabwe, explained to us the extremely unbearable situation of hunger, lost jobs, and torture by the government in Zimbabwe with Robert Mugabe's dictatorship. He spoke with uncontrollable emotion, with anger and excitement and his eyes were closed many times during conversation.

"I am in Botswana. I can speak loudly and freely about the situation in Zimbabwe," and he continued, "Now we have eighty percent unemployment, there is no democratic government; our only government is a corrupt one by Robert Mugabe, who is a cruel dictator". Again without stopping, "Presidential election is only for Robert Mugabe, no alternative choice candidate. People that speak against the government - a couple of days later or a couple of months later, they are gone without a trace or a single clue."

Bob from Oklahoma interrupted, "A Presidential election should be under the supervision of an electoral committee from the U.N."

"Robert Mugabe would not allow any committee from the U.N., and one more difficult thing is Robert Mugabe has a very good personal relationship with the nations surrounding Zimbabwe," was Tenash's quick response.

"Eighty percent unemployment is the right number, Tenash? With high unemployment, how can the people live?" That was the question from Jeff from California indicating eighty percent number is unbelievable.

Eighty percent. Wow! I could not believe it. I have heard twenty – twenty five percent of unemployment in Portugal, Spain and Greece. *I cannot believe eighty percent is the unemployment number* I mumbled to myself, "In the U.S. with over nine percent unemployment rate, we are screaming against the government policy on its tedious progress of reducing the unemployment rate and economic recovery."

"Yes. Eighty percent is the right number. Almost everybody is looking for a job to put food on the table." Tenash continued, "Zimbabwe was the richest country among our neighbors, Angola, Botswana and Zambia. Now it is quite different from the past, our people immigrate to Botswana and Zambia to look for jobs." It was shocking news to me. I thought just people from Mexico came to the U.S. and North Koreans to China looking for jobs and opportunities.

"Change the leader. That's simple," Bob shouted with his right hand up in the air, how can we change the Robert Mugabe government to a democratic society, with only thirteen people in our group. *No way*. I mumbled. We understood one hundred percent Tenash's explosion of anger and his desire to tell us the unbearable awkward situation in his country.

I have thought about Korea, past and present. We went through a similar situation to Zimbabwe, after the thirty six years of occupation by Japan, liberation in 1945 after World War II, and trying to build a democratic society like America, but Koreans did not have the experience in a democratic system. Koreans were controlled by the kingdom for over four thousand years and the last kingdom was for five hundred years under the Rhee dynasty.

During the Japanese occupation only a very tiny group had a chance for a high school education. Japan did not allow Koreans to go to college and treated them as second class citizens. The Korean young men were in the front lines of the battlefield or worked in coalmines.

After World War II, in 1945, the liberation from Japan, Korea had to build a free and democratic society, but the words of freedom and democratic society were new to our fathers' generation. They are only accustomed to Confucianism and Japanese occupation. With this thought, I told Tenash, "It will take time to have a democratic society without corruption," and added, "Korea took the same route, it was a long way to come to so-called democratic government with freedom of speech and without corruption."

We could not continue with more discussion, because our drivers and local guides waited for us for the evening game viewing.

The next day again over tea and cookies Tenash brought up a really touchy subject. First he hesitated even to bring up this one. We were getting more anxious to get involved with the issues. He consulted for a few moments with the local guides and got his courage up and he started the story.

How many elephants do you think are in Chobe National Park?" He asked. I thought he was playing number games. At the initial briefing, he told us one hundred twenty thousand elephants lived in Chobe National Park (fourteen thousand six hundred sixty eight square miles). Even I knew the numbers. I did not say, and quietly waited for the next movement. Without considering the issues, ladies screamed, "Elephants are cute, so cute". Then Dawn added, "Especially the baby elephant, she was always under the mom's belly". "Yes, so cute. I like them," Joan added this comment. Tenash cut the conversation, "Yes, they are cute but they are one of the five dangerous animals".

Dawn was kind of irritated and requested, "What are the five dangerous animals?"

"They are elephants, of course, leopards, lions, rhinos and hippos."

Everybody was quiet.

Bob could not wait, "What is the issue with elephants?"

"Do you remember that the population of elephants in Chobe National Park is about one hundred twenty thousand in the small park," Tenash continued, "Overpopulated elephants are damaging farm animals with limited food source. They are threatening the other animals' survival."

Bob quietly continued, "Kill them". His wife, Pat, nudged her husband to indicate, "Shut up. Killing is not an option," and she was extremely upset about killing the animals, especially the cute elephants. Then Tenash told us "The elephants are social animals. It is not easy to kill them. If you kill the mother, their siblings, even grandchildren, take revenge on the people or animals who killed their family. Elephants also have very, very special memories. If you transfer the elephant one hundred miles away from here, they will return somehow to the same location and they remember who did harm to their family."

"There is no real answer. Then what is your government's plan for an easy, quick, economical way to reduce the number of elephants?" April from Hawaii asked Tenash, because the long unsolved discussion bored or irritated her.

I could see Tenash's hesitation because he understood that many Americans are animal lovers and killing them is not an option, absolutely not.

"The government of Botswana thinks killing the elephants is the only way to reduce the numbers in a quick and economical way."

Nobody commented, but everybody was in agreement with the government's plan about killing eighty thousand elephants to reduce three-fourths of the population and setting up a slaughter plant. Meat can be used for food for people or animals. Elephant skins can be used for luxurious handbags or clothes and the ivory can be exported for special jewelry or ornaments. The economical boost in Botswana would be tremendous. Then slowly biological control of the elephant population through diet and birth control can be the solution. I agreed more than one hundred percent but I could not say so loudly because they are so cute, especially the image of the baby elephant under the mommy's belly sucking milk was in my heart.

Figure 84 Elephant with Baby

Figure 85 Elephant with Baby

Victoria Falls

The last tent lodge in Hwange National Park in Zimbabwe was a one hour and fifty minute flight to Victoria Falls in Zimbabwe. It was a small airplane, a thirteen seat Cessna. The runway was hardened sand. Luckily the soil was hard enough so a small airplane could land and lift over. By car it would have been five - six hours for the same distance.

The huge Hwange National Park has trees on the sand and was similar to the decoration of green dots on white canvas. The curved rivers were running through the park like a snake path. When we were near the city of Victoria Falls, about thirty miles away, the pilot told us, look at the middle of the field on the left side through the window.

"White clouds are coming out from the ground. Can you see it?"

"Yes. Yes," all of us screamed.

"That's Victoria Falls, like a hot springs is coming out from the ground."

We all looked at the small object far away among the green fields. In a short moment I was confused and forgot I was in the sky and above the falls and I thought the famous Victoria Falls comes from the tall mountain by dumping a tremendous amount of water into the bottom of the river. But the falls do not flow from the mountain. It is coming from the Zimbabwe River with several routes. Then the water dumps into the deep gorge.

By arriving at the small airport at Victoria Falls we could not escape the pouring rain, which is typical African weather. Today we were extremely lucky that we flew through the beautiful blue sky and occasionally through the white clouds belt.

Our local guide came and greeted us with several umbrellas and raincoats. The main guide, Tanesh, was on the way, a 5-6 hour drive by car, from the tent lodge and would arrive at 9:00 p.m. tonight. After a quick safety briefing at the lodge and unloading our luggage, the local guide did not waste any time starting the tour around Victoria Falls. Meanwhile the pouring rain was changing to drizzle. Our ponchos or a light raincoat was perfect for the tour. The lodge hotel was located inside the beautiful Victoria Falls Park with a regular wooden building, but still in the hotel room we had a mosquito net around the bed. The beautiful view from our room left me speechless. Trees, birds, mainly huge vultures, and impalas were running among the tropical forests. It was a paradise of animals.

It was only a twenty minute drive from the hotel to Victoria Falls National Park. Under the drizzling rain we started our tour around the falls. The local guide was so eager to show the falls and the statue of Dr. Livingstone in the park entrance. His long legs were hopping like a kangaroo. We all tried to keep up with his pace.

"Please, close to me. Just one thing I would like to emphasize about Dr. Livingstone," the guide did not stop talking about Dr. Livingstone whether we were close to his statue or not. "Even though his body is in England, his heart is in Zimbabwe, I should say in Africa, especially we could say in our hearts." The guide concluded the life of Dr. Livingstone as described above. ("His heart is in Africa"). We all listened quietly in front of the statue while we were hearing the thunderous waterfall.

The guide could not stop. "One more thing, everybody remember Dr. Livingstone's famous "Three C's?" I did, because I read his biography before our journey, but I was quiet.

"Yes. The famous Three C's are: Civilization, Christianity and Commercialization," and the guide continued, "That's the reason we have over eighty percent Christians in Zimbabwe."

"The scenery of the Victoria Falls, please, just follow the route and viewpoints along the falls. If you do not follow the route, it's very slippery, and you will fall into the gorge. We will never see you again. It will take about one and one-half - two hours to stop at all the viewpoints. Then just the closing time of the park is at 6:00 p.m. and we will end up at the same entrance we came in." The guide did not miss one more thing. "The mist of falls is like raindrops. Be careful about your camera. Also, if you have plastic bags, that's great for protection for your camera. It's very slippery. Be careful".

It was very hard for me to imagine and understand the journey of Dr. Livingstone in the 1890's with no roads, mosquito bites, snakes and wild animals. He traveled across the wild dark continent and spent many decades sacrificing his life to educate the people in Africa's dark age. With his warm heart and Christianity, he respected their primitive and beautiful traditions.

Also, one more time I thought about the very meaningful story of the initial meeting with Dr. Livingstone and the famous American journalist, Henry Morton Stanley, who was looking for Dr. Livingstone's whereabouts, since communication with Dr. Livingstone had stopped for several years in his later life. "Dr. Livingstone, I presume." This is Stanley's famous first phrase from his mouth when he saw Dr. Livingstone who was sick with malaria.

After we left the statue of Dr. Livingstone we arrived at the first viewpoint. The mist is pouring all over our raincoats. The wide, thick water stream from the riverbank was falling down with loud thunder. The water volume is more than Niagara Falls and about one hundred meters high, which is twice that of Niagara Falls.

It's a stunning view, "a thunder of water". For a moment I thought *I am so glad I came here. For the Victoria Falls alone, it is worthwhile to be in Zimbabwe* then I was busy wiping the lens of the camera and eyeglasses. While we moved on to the next stations we had more and more mist from water drops, like having pouring rain again. About one and one-half miles distance a couple of dozen streams made thunderous falls with unbearable raindrops, impossible to take any more pictures. Our shoes and pants below the knees were totally wet, which attached themselves to our skin.

In Angel Falls in Venezuela, one stream is coming down from one thousand meters high. In Iguazu Falls in Brazil, water is coming down from several branches of river streams, and Niagara Falls is on the border of Canada and the USA. The grand scale of the Victoria Falls' water volume and height cannot compare to any of these falls that I had visited. *"Yes. It is magnificent,"* and I continued to mumble, *"It is a wonder of nature and the people of Zimbabwe and Zambia are chosen people to have such natural wonders that are part of God's creation."*

Kwang still tried to have a Kodak moment to take a picture of the falls and me in each station with his soaked camera.

More than half of our group gave up on finishing all fourteen viewpoints. They had the perfect reason to quit, because the mist prohibited seeing the falls and we could not take any pictures unless the camera was waterproof. A more dangerous issue was the road was extremely slippery.

But Kwang and I, with two other young ladies were hopping station by station until the last spot, near the famous bridge between Zimbabwe and Zambia. Many years ago Zimbabwe and Zambia were one country as Rhodesia, named for Cecil Rhodes when the bridge was built in the period of Rhodesia.

Kwang and I spent almost two hours hopping around the view points, one by one. When we came out the gate (entrance) our group was waiting at the bar with dry clothes.

So far the Victoria Falls means a great volume of water with "thunder of smoke" or "thunder of water" and the statue honoring Dr. Livingstone's memory into eternity at Victoria Falls over the rainbow.

Figure 86 Victoria Falls

Figure 87   Victoria Falls

Figure 88 At the Victoria Falls

African Termite Mounds

In the middle of December 2011, Kwang and I had a chance to have a safari in Botswana, Zambia and Zimbabwe. We stayed in a tent lodge in a national park during our trip, such as Chobe National Park in Botswana, Kafue National Park in Zambia and Hwange National Park in Zimbabwe

At least twice daily we had game viewing through the park by driving four wheel open trucks to look for exciting animal behavior. Hopefully, we would see the excitement of a cheetah chasing a leopard or a lion – or baboon that just gave birth. But nothing like these extremely unusual events was happening. We just saw lazy lion families lying down in the bush and baby cheetahs looking at us with curiosity from the nearby main road. Baboons were holding babies affectionately or they carried their babies on their backs, swinging around on the tree branches.

African national parks consist of dense tropical forest and endless savannah areas like green lakes in the forest and, of course, wild animals, such as giraffes, elephants, wild dogs, zebras, lions, leopards, impalas and birds. In addition to this scenery, we saw unique and unusual sculptures with the color of gray and white in the vast green savannahs.

You might confuse these objects with beautiful headstones in a cemetery when you see them from a far distance, but they are African termite mounds. Since we were not allowed to step on the ground from the truck, we looked at the termite mounds that stood near the road where we were driving, and then had a chance to take pictures. Some are very small, one foot high and one-half foot round with a simple design like an ice cream cone. Some are more than ten feet high and five foot round, with indescribable designs. Some are more detailed than a Michelangelo sculpture, and many are abstract sculptures, more appealing than a Picasso. All varieties of these termite mounds represented the artistic work of termites, such as the beautiful and magnificent castles, a handsome and strong man, a mysterious smile on a Mona Lisa face and the long trunk of an elephant on the green savannah. I took pictures of almost every termite mound on the roadside.

"Why are you taking so many pictures of termite mounds?" Kwang asked me in a grumpy voice.

"It's fascinating. Look at that one. It's like a castle on the sand," and I continued, "The guide told us it will take many years to make a five foot high termite mound," and continued, "It's really astonishing, such small creatures building mounds like these. Unbelievable."

Kwang was quiet because of my strong opinion and excitement over the termite mounds.

"Kwang, I will write a story about African termite mounds," I concluded.

"Kook-Wha, maybe there are tons of stories about termite mounds. What is new about yours?" Kwang asked. "Whether mine will be new or not, I will write about what I saw and what I experienced with them," I responded. We were quiet. There was a cold war starting between us again. The head guide did not give us much information about the termite mounds. His priority was spotting lions, cheetahs and, hopefully, rhinos, instead of small creatures like termites.

I looked in the travel guidebook and Kwang's collected information on termite mounds. They all showed beautiful and unique sculptures with little stories about how the mounds are built by termites.

The first and only time we had a chance to walk through the park was at Hwange National Park in Zimbabwe. We walked for about three hours with an extremely experienced local guide. Six people joined him. The guide was about seventy years old and has four wives, but is still walking and running like a forty or fifty year old, and had forty years experience as a guide with the national park.

After about a twenty minute drive from the lodge, we started to walk inside the wild African tropical forest. "Everybody walk together and close to each other. You never know, we may have a strange encounter," the local guide warned us. I noticed that he had a gun and also an axe. "Will you shoot animals with your gun?" Bob from Oklahoma asked him. "No. There are no bullets in this gun." "Then why did you bring it?" I criticized him sharply. "Just for security," the guide answered. *No bullets – for security?* That was odd, I thought.

While walking through the tropical forest in the park he showed us how we could make a toothbrush from the trees and the application of medicinal leaves and trees for stomach ache and fevers. We saw the amazing small creatures, such as the beetle. Beetles rolled on elephant dung, making balls in the sandy area.

So far we have not had any animal encounters. Even the early morning sunbeams were hitting us and we all wanted to sit down on the ground in the shade and everybody was looking for drinking water.

We came to a small termite mound, two and one-half feet high and the bottom is about one and one-half feet wide and the top was about one-half foot in diameter with whitish gray color. "Come close to me around this termite mound. It's a small one, but very interesting," the guide was excited to start talking.

"It's active?" Kwang asked him, because nothing was moving and it looked like it was made of white sand or concrete.

"Yes. Look at this," then the guide kicked the top of the mound and spread the sand. Then the small termites were crawling everywhere around the ground.

"Oh! Oh!" everybody was frightened that the termites might crawl up their legs. "Termites are useful creatures. Both animals and human beings eat termites. It's a delicacy and a good protein source," the guide continued.

"They are so tiny and very small," I added.

"Yes, but it's tasty," then the guide put a couple of termites on his tongue and ate them. "Taste it. It's good," he offered some to me to try. When he put them in his mouth, I closed my eyes. When I opened my eyes, I saw two termites were still on his tongue and several termites were on his palm.

It was alive, very tiny, light brownish color, about the size of an ant. I hesitated, then took it and swallowed it, as a vitamin pill or small baby aspirin. "There is no taste. Too small," I commented. "Some sour taste?" the guide asked me. "No. I could not taste any." He emphasized again that it is a good protein source and a delicacy in Africa and explained more about various applications for termite mounds. The information is all new to me; my knowledge was limited to termites gnawing the wood in house structures.

"The termite mounds in Africa can rise to heights of over thirty feet by such a small creature," the guide started to explain.

"Wow." We all echoed (screamed).

"It's quite a tall building," I said and the guide nodded and continued," Termites contribute to a great extent to our ecosystems as decomposers of wood and plant debris. They aerate the soil of the savannah and add nutrients to it."

"Add nutrients to soil? I do not understand," Kwang asked.

"Not only nutrients to soil, but they are a good food source for animals, including man as I told you," and the guide continued, "Termite mounds have a fantastic ventilation system, a hollow tube in the middle which circulates hot and cold air. The chemicals secreted by termites are used for road construction and makes the materials cheaper and more durable than asphalt," he continued. *Amazing phenomena of nature* I mumbled.

He continued, "Termites dig deep into the earth in search of water. They can go down farther than two hundred feet, and all that soil is brought up to ground level and added to the structure of the mound. For this reason, ore is mixed into the termite mound. The soil of the mound can be inspected by geologists to see what lies deeper in the earth. Gold prospectors are known to inspect termite mounds. In fact, the largest diamond mine in the world, in Botswana, was discovered by examining a termite mound."

We spent most of the time, about one and one-half hours, reviewing fascinating stories about African termite mounds and we headed to the edge of the park through the dead trees which had fallen down. We were warm, soaked with sweat, and, without seeing any snakes or any wild animals, we arrived at our truck. We only saw insects, beetles and termites.

Figure 89 Termite Mound

Figure 90 Termite Mound

Figure 91 On Termite Mound

Moroccan Tagine and Mint Tea

In February 2012, in order to escape from the bitter cold and snowy days in Detroit, Michigan, Kwang and I spent a couple of weeks in Morocco, Africa, which is on the coast line of the Mediterranean Sea and the Atlantic Ocean with the Tour Group Cosmos. Before my writing directly about the Moroccan cuisine, Tagine and Mint Tea, I would like to briefly highlight the route we took during our two weeks in Morocco.

When we arrived in Casablanca, we were amazed that the famous "Rick's Café Americain" movie location from "Casablanca", with Humphrey Bogart and Ingrid Bergman, was there and I began to whistle and hum my favorite song, "As Time Goes By". The Royal Palace and Hassan Tower were unforgettable buildings in Casablanca, but we did not spend much time in this city and our tour continued to Rabat, the capital city of Morocco. The beautiful royal palace, Chellah gate walls and garden of Oudaia, Hassan tower and mausoleum and the tomb of Mohammad V made a great impression on me in Rabat.

The next stop was Meknes, the famous Tomb of Ismael Moulay, and all the pieces in the buildings in Meknes were beautiful mosaics.

The colorful souks in old Medina in Fez were in a small alley which has thousands of shops and was an extremely challenging adventure for us. It was a trick to find the same entrance where we came in. Seven Gates royal palace and Karauine Mosque were magnificent, but since I saw many mosques and palaces, they all looked alike. In Fez, they have the unique leather industry, colorful leather slippers, jackets and handbags to offer the temptation of purchasing products. If I did not have a leather jacket, I would buy at least one, maybe two. In order to avoid giving Kwang a heart attack, I only bought one pair of black slippers for him, even though he did not want them, I told him, "It's a souvenir for you." He walked away from me without any comment.

From the second floor where the shop was located, we could see thousands of different dying vats on the ground without any cover in the open air. It was Saturday and nobody was working at the dying process vats, the myriad colors and smells jammed our senses.

After Fez, we passed the town of Ifrane which was built by the French in the middle Atlas region.   And as we crossed the middle Atlas range to Midelt after we passed the fortified mud and straw villages with flat roofs, a green cedar forest led to volcanic mountains. We descended further into the spectacular Ziz Gorge and arrived in Er Rachindia.

The stunning view of white snow and sledding and downhill skiing at the high Atlas Mountain was unexpected. I expected it to be much warmer in Morocco than in Detroit.

Er Rachindia was an important crossroads and was once controlled by the French Foreign Legion. Afterwards, the landscape became progressively more arid and we traveled through a stony desert to Erford, which has the breathtaking scenery like a peaceful oasis of the Ziz Valley.

In Erford that evening my camel riding experience in the Sahara Desert was unbelievably fantastic. We climbed up to the Sahara desert on the saddles of camels. Watching the scenery, on my right the sun was going down with burning red colors and on my left the cold full moon was up already in the middle of the sky. It was a memory that I would take with me forever. After riding we rested for a few minutes on the edge of the desert hill in order to watch the day become night. As the sun sank into the desert floors, I held Kwang's hand and told him, "How lucky we are, at our age we can travel with much younger people, even riding camels in the Sahara Desert without any problems." Kwang nodded.

The sands were more coarse and brown than in the Gobi Desert in Mongolia, but the camel riding to the middle of the sand dune for about one hour was a big event for our group. "Kwang, this is like we were crossing the 'Silk Road'".

"Yes, it is. Maybe they did use this route thousands of years ago," Kwang spoke with a great deal of excitement.

Before I arrived in Morocco I did not know that Moroccan oranges and tangerines are famous in the world, juicy, fresh, not too small, and not too big. One other famous produce was dates from Tineghir Oasis palm trees covered with palms among red mud-straw houses with flat roofs.

When we arrived at Quarzazate, the film capital in Morocco, we found out that the actual location for the film "Casablanca" was in Hollywood, U.S.A. When the guide told us this on the bus, we were disappointed a great deal, "Oh, no. That could not be true!"

Before returning to Casablanca again, the last stop was Marrakesh, known as "the pearl of the south" in Morocco, which is one of Morocco's imperial cities and the second oldest city in the country. There we discovered the original Djemaa el-Fna Square, Saadian Tombs and El Bahia Palace, all glorious ancient monuments to history. Inside the alley of the Djemaa el Fna Square are a thousand shops with spices, leather products, wicker works and embroidery. It was hard to avoid purchasing some of these beautiful and unique products from Morocco, especially from these alleys. "Let's go," Kwang pulled my arm and kept me away from the shops. "Just look at it, don't buy," he warned me again and made me grumpy. Still he was dragging me. *Right. He is right* but I did not say that to him. *Right, there is too much junk in my closet*"

We returned to Casablanca and the famous Hassan II mosque close to the Atlantic Ocean. The mosque was constructed two thirds over the water inspired by two verses of the Koran stating, "The Throne of God was Upon the Waters" and "From Water Have We Created All Life". The Hassan II Mosque, we were told, is the tallest religious building in the world and the second largest in the Muslim world, after the Al Haramayan Acharifian Mosque in Mecca. After the death of His Royal Highness, King Mohammed V in 1961, his son, Hassan II built the building as a mausoleum for his father. Situated in the extreme northwest point of what Muslims call Dar Al Islam (the land of Islam), the mosque proffers itself as a meeting point for the diverse cultures of the African, European, Mediterranean and Arab nations.

The mosque covers nine hectares and is two thirds in the water. The craftsmanship of the walls and domes, especially one of the domes in the prayer room, is almost beyond description with beautiful mosaics. The nighttime scene of the mosque has grandeur and beauty, reminiscent of when I was young, reading "The Arabian Nights / One Thousand and One Nights". *I almost expected to hear Scheherazade telling stories to the sultan.*

In Rabat, Casablanca, Marrakesh and other cities, Tagines and Mint Teas were our quick lunch. Tagine is a Berber tribal name for a dish from North Africa, named after the special earthenware pot in which it is cooked.

Now is the time I would like to describe the Tagine and Mint Tea ceremony. It consists of two parts: a base unit that is flat and circular with low sides, and a large cone or dome shaped cover that sits on the base during cooking. The cover is designed to promote the return of all condensation to the bottom. With the cover removed, the base can be taken to the table. To me it looked like a small cone shaped distillation column. The same principle applies here as in a chemistry lab, with all the condensation returning to the bottom of the flask. I was told the cover can be removed without a mitten or hot pad. But I wouldn't want to try it, for fear of burning myself. *What a clever idea with a scientific principle!!*

Tagine is slow cooked, braised at low temperature with less expensive meats, such as lamb, neck, shoulder or shank, cooked until it is falling off the bone. Lamb is not the only meat. Others used are chicken, beef, turkey and fish, and additional ingredients like dates, apples, pears, raisins, prunes, nuts or preserved or fresh lemons. It is just like a stew in our country, but the cookware is for each individual person. Tagine was served with thin pizza dough type of bread with mint tea. It was delicious because the cookware kept the temperature warm until we finished it. Tagine at lunch time is like quick fast food from McDonald's or Burger King in the United States, but far more interesting and healthy.

Several Tagines in brownish red clay pots lined up over a charcoal fire for waiting guests. Kwang stuck to having beef meatball Tagine, which wasn't as imaginative as my chicken and lamb with vegetables and dates. The warm Tagines were absolutely delicious.

Moroccan mint tea is green tea with sugar or without sugar with mint leaves in the tiny glass (about fifty milliliters) and tea was filled to about one third of the cup. Mint tea with a meal, or all day long is served as the drink of hospitality, usually served whenever there are guests. Unlike Moroccan food, cooked by women, this tea is traditionally a man's affair; prepared by the head of the family with a tea ceremony in front of the guests. When it is served to guests, it is impolite to refuse it. The green tea comes from China and the preparation of mint tea is quite a ceremony of art. We enjoyed watching the tea pouring from a distance of fifteen to twenty inches high to produce the foam in the glass without spilling a drop of tea outside of the glass. A tea ceremony was held at the carpet store by the owner of the store.

The host sat on the floor in front of the small round table about one foot high which contained two beautiful teapots, small decorative glasses, fresh mint leaves, dried green tea leaves, sugar and boiling water. He rinsed the tea pots with boiling water, then added the tea leaves to each pot and rinsed them with small boiling water. The water was discarded. Sugar was added in the tea pots and he filled them with boiling water. The tea was allowed to steep for several minutes before being stirred and then he filled the tea glasses. While we drank our first glasses of tea, he replenished the pots with more tea leaves and sugar. He also added fresh mint leaves. This was the second pot of tea, and then on to the third pot.

Our host recited the following famous Moroccan proverb when we finished the second glass:

"The first glass is as bitter as life

The second glass is as strong as love

The third glass is as gentle as death."

We all burst into laughter and left.

It was a free tea ceremony and glasses of mint tea, but, unfortunately, mint tea was charged as an extra drink at the restaurant.

Figure 92   Moroccan Tagine

Figure 93   In front of Tagine Store

Figure 94   Tagine in a Shop

Figure 95   Pretty Tagine

SOUTH AMERICA

Darwin's Place, Galapagos Islands

Even if we had plenty of connection time from Panama City to Quito, Ecuador, the main entrance to the Galapagos Islands, Panama airlines could not provide the connections. They just informed us, "The plane left already". We were angry. "Departure time is 7:00 p.m. It is now 5:35 p.m." The lady at the ticket counter acted like she didn't or couldn't understand us. "It is unbelievable that the plane left before the departure time," I complained, even though nobody was listening, "Just talking to the wall."

We stayed over in a small hotel in Panama City without any given definite schedule for departure to Quito. The girl at the counter had murmured that the first flight would be at 7:00 p.m. tomorrow evening. "7:00 p.m. or 7:00 a.m.?" I could not believe what she said. I repeated "7:00 p.m.?" She repeated it vaguely "7:00 p.m." Thirty to forty people stayed at the hotel near the airport arranged by the airlines' counter. One third from this group was English speaking and the remainder was native South American. Nobody complained. People seemed to accept it as the normal routine. I was the only one? I was furious.

A young biology student named Kim from the University of Houston, Houston, Texas, was one of the passengers. I grabbed him for his assistance or just to be together, since he could speak English and Spanish. Surprisingly, he was Korean, studying in Texas and living in Quito. His father has been in the oil business in Quito for more than ten years and he had spent his childhood in Quito. It is quite an odd, interesting and international life. I thought, *It is too bad, he only has two legs; he should have three or four legs, like a mini-octopus to connect him to several different countries.*

The squeaking bed in the hotel room woke me up whenever I turned around, but Kwang began snoring a long time before. For a couple of hours, I just looked at the ceiling with a gray spider web dangling at the corner. The small fluorescent light was enough to find my way to the bathroom. I could not sleep. I still had deep, bitter feelings about the way we had been treated at the airport.

I woke Kwang up and discussed strategy for tomorrow. "We cannot wait until 7:00 p.m. tomorrow evening. We would lose the whole day's excursion from our group." He was quiet, half asleep and half awake. He did not have any definite plans and neither did I.

"Kwang, we did not ask Mr. Kim what his plans are. He should know what to do because he is almost local here." I continued, "It's better to wait at the airport. It cannot be just one airplane daily from Panama City to Quito. I think at least two or three daily." "Hmmm." He gave a deep sigh and then he was quiet again. We were lucky enough that the hotel floor did not sink with his heavy sigh. "Let's go to the airport and wait there for the earliest or first flight before 7:00 p.m.," I demanded.

Kwang followed my strong and unavoidable orders and, using the taxi in front of the hotel, we arrived at the airport around 6:00 a.m. We rushed to the airline counter to request a standby for the first flight. Five minutes later Mr. Kim was behind us and five to ten minutes later about one-half of our group of forty people were in the line. "Aha. This way it does work," I commented and continued, "What would have happened if we stayed at the hotel until 7:00 p.m.?" Unfortunately, we could not make the first flight, which took most of the local people, including Mr. Kim who knew the rules for normal service of the airlines in Quito.

About five or ten of us took the second flight around 10:00 a.m. by purchasing new tickets. They did not honor the old tickets for standby even if we did not use them; this was a rule unheard of and a most disgusting experience in Panama City.

We arrived at Quito around noon and needed another short hop from Quito to the Galapagos Islands. From the island, we had to chase a small cruise liner that was our main tour boat. Luckily the lady from our G.A.P. travel group arranged all the connections to the Galapagos Islands but we had to pay again for everything in cash. Hiring a private speedboat to chase our main tour boat for two hours cost $650.00.

An eighteen foot long white motorboat was operated by an old man with short, but strong muscles, thick gray hair, and short pants. He could not speak any English and we could not speak any Spanish. He was in the driver's seat and we were on back bench. Fortunately he received precise instructions from the G.A.P. travel agent.

No life jackets, strange I murmured. Even in our small sailboats we carry life jackets all the time. "The Ecuadorian people swim like fish, maybe," Kwang mentioned with a smile on his face. "Fish do not need life jackets," I responded and we both laughed.

Two days struggle at the airport left me exhausted, like I was in the battlefield in Iraq under the sizzling sun. On the bench in the boat a nice breeze was flowing through my body under beautiful blue sky. Once on the azure water, the relaxing feeling I could not compare with anything else. The driver maneuvered with moderate speed near the shore and channels but when we came to the middle of the ocean the speed of the boat was unimaginable. The bottom did not seem to touch the water, we flew so fast. The propeller pumped out water from the boat like a dam was pushing the water out for electricity. I moved from the bench and lay down in the bottom of the boat.

The driver told us it would take about two hours to catch our main boat, but I was concerned. "Kwang, at this speed can we get there in less than two hours?" "I do not know." His answer was monotonous and his expression showed no interest at all in how long it would take to catch up.

"This is like super high speed chasing, like going after drug dealers in Ecuador. It is absolutely scary," I added.

"Yes. I hope the bottom of the boat doesn't crack. With the hammering sounds of water, the bottom of the boat could not last long." My response was the same as his concern. "How many hours left to arrive at our boat?" I asked Kwang with fear. "By his word, we still have one more hour to go."

Kwang's quiet voice disappeared with the engine noise and the waves of water.

"Another hour. No problem." My tenacious and strong mind could hold me for one more hour. "No problem." Just please, do not feel seasick and do not crack the bottom of the boat. I talked to myself and closed my eyes with my right hand. Water vapor and drops were falling on my face from the back of the boat like a drizzling spring rain.

When we arrived at our main boat, it was already late afternoon. Our group of sixteen people was assigned to eight cabins. The boat was relatively small, like a big houseboat. The cabins were downstairs, and the dining area was on the upper deck. With this small boat, we could sail the narrow canals among several islands.

The Galapagos Islands are six hundred miles west of Ecuador and consist of nineteen islands. We visited only nine islands for a ten day trip: Baltra, Espanola, El Progreso, Rabida, Santa Rosa, Santa Cruz, Santa Fe, Santiago and Seymour. The youngest island is two hundred fifty years old. Each island has a different soil and different species of life, with seals on every island. In such a small area, many different species exist without fear of human intruders.

"Astonishing phenomenon, Kwang. I think I can understand Darwin's evolution theory."

"Yes. I am glad we came, even after all the hassle."

It's different remembering which animals are on which island but one island stands out among the rugged volcanic rocks there was one very narrow passage, with no trace of a trail. Golden brown iguanas and gray, dark ones lay on the rocks everywhere and staring at us without moving. Not only the iguanas, the seals do not run away either. They just stayed where they were or moved around wherever they wanted to go, without hurry or fear.

First I just looked at their slim tails, feet and heads from a long distance. They were so ugly like alligators and my skin crawls just at the remembrance of snakes and alligators, but since I could approach them closer than the normal distance, I could see the beautiful shining mosaic type golden skin and the glistening eyes were trying to focus on objects. My fears of looking at them and my feelings of discomfort were diminishing.

"What kind of psychology of these animals? It is very unique. Kwang, can you explain why the animals are not afraid of us and just stay there. Is it great for us to take a photo?" I asked Kwang. "Maybe they have not had the life and death threat before. They just live here peacefully with great harmony among the different species," Kwang added to my comment.

"A tall, huge cactus stood among the volcanic rocks on one island out of the nineteen, but all the rest of them consist of volcanic rocks," I continued. "The youngest one is two hundred fifty years old, but the volcano might erupt at any time and make one more island," Kwang concluded and added, "We have to go to the beach for snorkeling for our next excursion".

Baby seals were sucking milk from their mother's belly on the sand. I tried to get as close as possible to get a special, unique photo. I have never seen four baby seals sucking milk from their mother. It could be a great picture that I could hand down as a family treasure from generation to generation. They did not move and I got closer and closer. Suddenly the mother turned around and tried chasing me. I fell down with my camera. I scrambled backwards crablike. The mother seal was moving faster than I thought. "Stupid". "Be careful." Kwang was beside me. "You tried to catch a unique picture, too." I talked back to him in a grumpy voice.

Now I had to remember Hinan, our guide, advised us on the first day that "The animals on the Galapagos Islands will not hurt you or attack you, but do not get too close to them. You never know."

In some areas the volcanic rocks on the beach are pitch black. Some are huge and some are flat enough that I could step on the rocks. "Kook-Wha, be careful. There are many crabs on the rocks," our guide Hinan screamed at me. He did not say it, but he implied, "Kook-Wha, you already made enough trouble on the beach, please be careful". "Yes. I will." I shouted back at him. Then I could see the red crabs on the black rocks. "Yuck. Red crabs are all over."

"Yes. Those are called Christmas crabs." Hinan continued, "Kook-Wha, they will bite you and they are much faster than you and there is a possibility that they will crawl on your body." "Yes. I will." Again I answered back to him. The Christmas crabs are so beautiful, bright, real bright red color was on the black rocks, crawling all over the rocks and some were taking it easy, taking a nap. Usually the gray color crabs turned into a red-orange color when we boiled them, but these crabs are live ones with red color. They are absolutely beautiful on the black rocks.

"That's enough. Let's move on to the end of the island to see the special bird which lives only in the Galapagos Islands." Hinan continued, "Do you know what it is?" "Blue footed booby" a young college student proudly answered. "Yes. It is the blue-footed booby. They are only in the Galapagos Islands." About one hundred yards away from the residence of Christmas crabs, there is a cliff on the Pacific Ocean. Occasional white waves make a unique design on the dark blue ocean and a spout of water is blowing out periodically about one hundred yards to the sky so-called "blown holes".

Two blue-footed boobies sat on a small trail near the cliff and were watching the people passing by. They did not fly away, they just sat there. "Kwang, they do not know how to fly like the kiwi in Australia." "Be quiet. They might fly away." He nudged my left side. "They were just photogenic," Hinan added. A foot long body has a white breast and gray and black feathers around her body but beautiful light blue feet. Also, compared to other birds, the feet are wider and the bones are connected with membrane, like ducks, and they have a long sharp beak that can catch fish in the ocean. Afterwards they showed us their beautiful blue feet like a fashion show and flew away to the ocean and dove into the water to catch fish.

We turned around and headed back to our main boat. Suddenly Hinan stopped us and with his hands stretching behind him indicated that "be quiet," Hinan ordered urgently. "Be quiet and don't move. This is a very rare case at the Christmas season. The Albatross have already left the Galapagos Islands and usually would come back next spring. Maybe this couple is the last one left," and again continued, "Look at their dancing." We could barely hear his low tense voice. "You guys are very lucky to see their dancing," Hinan continued. Now I could see what he meant, about ten yards away two albatross were dancing and kissing each other. The dancing rhythm seems like somebody is playing the drums for their dance. "It will last about an hour," Hinan continued.

The movement of feet and body and neck and head, it was almost impossible to describe. A beautiful kissing scene is to please each other. I had the temptation to kiss Kwang.

When we left the dancing scene, they continued to dance and kiss each other. It was really a rare occasion. We saw a beautiful scene. But at that time I did not ask if they dance with every partner or a special one, or if this is a special occasion for their mating season. Still I have not asked and I have not looked at the Internet.

The next morning we were in a pontoon, rubber boat, exploring the small channels with mangrove trees at the shore and connected small, tiny and large lagoons. Strangely enough, each lagoon has its own species of fish, gray sharks, huge green turtles were swimming around, frequently their heads popped up to look at us. The colorful tropical fish were busy swimming around chasing their own targets. The green turtles are huge, at least one yard long, three quarters yard wide of their hard shell. We could not see the small turtles but saw lots of big ones. We were told this particular area is the home of the golden stingray but nobody from our group saw one.

I am not a so-called environmentalist, but I started to be concerned about the Galapagos Islands, keeping them safe from intruders like us, doing irreversible damage on the islands. When we were in Antarctica, our boots were sanitized before leaving the boat for the Antarctic Peninsula, and one more time we sanitized our boots also before stepping on the land and we took the same procedure of sanitizing our boots before boarding the boat. Less than one hundred people are allowed to land on the Antarctic Peninsula at one time. In the Galapagos Islands there were no restrictions on the number of people or sanitization and several tour boats with several hundred people were on the ocean at the same time to tour the islands. This was a great concern and disturbance in order to keep the Galapagos Islands as Charles Darwin wanted to preserve them as evidence for his theory of evolution.

The next stop was the turtle farm. The land was not like a volcanic island. Some tropical trees and bushes were in the park. It was warm and humid in December. Hinan told us as soon as we were in five hundred hectares Galapagos National Park (or Turtle Farm), three – five thousand turtles live in the park. Some turtles are about two hundred fifty years old, some are younger than that. The turtles are everywhere, like chickens in a chicken coop or cows in the field.

With nobody watching them, about one yard long and three quarters yard wide, turtles with blackish color, long wrinkled necks, two strange black eyes and walking slowly everywhere, on the road, under the trees, in the mud, sometimes four or five together, or alone. They didn't seem frightened and didn't seem to care about the people surrounding them. If we were too close to them they just hid their ugly long necks inside their shells without any other movement. I had a temptation to touch the shell but I remembered that Hinan told us, "You never know, and respect the animals". We were all surprised at so many turtles living to such an old age, two hundred fifty years old, and we were strolling around the park for a couple of hours without tiring to see so many turtles in my life in one place.

Now we were ready to return to our main boat and came near the main entrance gate of the park. At the northwest corner, under the tree and near tree trunk, two turtles were mating. Step by step I was getting closer and closer to the turtles who were mating. *This is the greatest opportunity in my life to take a photo where turtles* are *having a good time.* I talked to myself. I was ten feet, eight feet, five feet away. I did not know Kwang was behind me. "No closer. That is close enough," he murmured. He took a picture and almost ran away. I did a click and "Oh", so relieved that I did it. Also a couple more people from our group took advantage of this rare occasion. Then we left the turtle farm. Again, these pictures will be a family treasure to pass on to our children.

"We saw many turtles, but how can three – five thousand turtles stay in this park?" one young man asked Hinan. "Some are on the beach for eggs but remember this park has 500 hectares. It is a huge park," Hinan explained. I was so satisfied that I whispered to Kwang, "Where can we see more than this spectacular scene?" "Yes. It is more than our expectations," Kwang answered.

"I will recommend our friends visit here before they get too old", I added to Kwang. "Maybe someday the tourism in the Galapagos Islands might be restricted in order to eliminate any irreversible environmental impact." Kwang expressed his concern, "Yes. That is one of the ways that we can comfort Darwin's soul and continue to study his evolution theory".

"Of course, if Panama Airlines continues it's nonsensical flight plans, few people will even get to visit Quito, much less the Galapagos Islands, unless they parachute in."

Figure 96　Iguana

Figure 97　Blue -footed Boobies

Figure 98 Chased away by baby seal

Figure 99 Two Iguanas

Figure 100　Iguana

Figure 101　Sailing around Galapagos Islands

Walking Under the Sea in Tahiti

After a late breakfast .we had plenty of time before our next excursion of walking under water. The mid-morning sun in Tahiti was hitting us with sizzling temperatures. I was confused that I was baking inside of an oven.

Instead of using our regular sailboat WindStar for today's excursion, we used a small two-deck motorboat which had a capacity of twenty people, for taking us for a walk under the sea.

The motorboat was cruising to the middle of the ocean. A most pleasant wind was touching my skin, leaving behind a black beach and hotels. My long hair was flying in the wind and I felt comfortable sitting on the deck. The motorboat stalled in the middle of the ocean for our excursion. Maybe it was five miles away from the beach. The sun was in the middle of the sky and the heat was unbearable and roasting me even for ten to fifteen minutes staying on the deck while the instructors were preparing for the excursion. "It is hot!" everybody echoed, wiping the sweat on their foreheads.

I jumped into the water and swam around the boat among the high waves. Everybody followed me into the water to cool down their body temperatures.

While our instructors, Liz and Bonnie, organized the equipment, we had to put sun tan lotion on again, even though we had put it on before we left the hotel, less than two hours ago. Liz and Bonnie wore big heavy oxygen tanks that must have weighed over thirty pounds. Each one had long plastic tubes connecting to the tank with their mouths instead of wearing heavy helmets like ours. They floated around the boat and then disappeared under water. We were told that the two instructors were professional scuba divers who usually went down one hundred feet.

They lay down the helmets which were connected to oxygen tanks. "Every attachment and control device is all set. You do not need to touch anything for any adjustments." Liz started to explain our excursion. "The helmet is a little heavy and uncomfortable the first time, but will be fine during our walk underwater," she continued. Then she gave us step-by-step procedures and instructions for wearing the helmet and safety rules.

"Our excursion is about one hour," added Bonnie. "That's all?" One of the young men complained.

"One hour is quite adequate and actually it is a long time under the water," Liz commented.

"We will be around you all the time under the sea. If you feel dizzy, let us know immediately," she continued. "Any questions?" Everybody was quiet. Strangely enough, there were no questions at all. Everybody seemed very comfortable about diving into the sea except me. I did not know what to ask. "Being under water with only an oxygen tank connected to a helmet is scary. *It is scary* with this thought, I also mumbled, *I had to get rid of this cowardly feeling.* "No questions? Then let's start," the instructors ordered in an energetic mood, and we all seemed to expect great things under the sea like a treasure hunt.

A total of six people joined. Three men, including Kwang, and three women (two of the women were in their early thirties) including me. I soon found out that all the people in our group were scuba divers except for Kwang and I. That's the reason we did not have any questions. We put our helmets on with assistance from the instructors.

The heavy rectangular helmet with a window in front of my face weighed maybe only ten pounds, but it felt like more than twenty pounds of rocks on my shoulders. There was very little space between the helmet and my eardrums. The gray colored helmet consisted of plastic shell with heavy weight inside. My first thought was, *Am I choking? No. I could breathe. I am ok. Can I get this helmet off after walking under water?* My second thought, *What if I stopped breathing?*

Two young men went down the stairs from the boat slowly into the water with helmets connected to oxygen tanks on their backs, and disappeared from the surface of the water. Then Kwang and I tried it. He did not have any fear and naturally he was anxious to go down into the sea. I was scared to death with the helmet on. It was tight and I could not move my neck. Even though I was breathing, I felt that there was no air. "Kwang, are you okay?" He did not answer me. He was too busy getting ready to go into the water, but I could not.

Liz and Kwang showed me with their hands that it would be okay. Kwang went down a couple of steps into the water and then he came back to the deck. After he saw my hesitation, he sat down beside me with the helmet. I shook my head. "I cannot. I am really scared. You go ahead." Four people were underwater and I could not see them anymore. Kwang was eager to follow the group and was struggling about whether to leave me on the deck and follow the group. He desperately wanted to go down. "Umm. Are you ready?" he asked me. "No. Not at all. I am so scared," was my answer. He was getting grumpy from the heat and eager to go down to the bottom.

"Kwang, you can go," I finally blurted out.

In my mind he should not go away from me on the deck. "Okay. I will go down. You can come later." As soon as he spoke those words he disappeared into the water. He seemed so glad that I let him go.

Everybody went down except Liz and I. For about ten minutes I thought that I had made the right decision. No regrets about staying on the deck. On the deck, the only scenery that was left was just waves, white and blue waves making wrinkles, coming and going.

The heat from the sun was making it more difficult to stay on the deck. I was debating about choosing new experiences under the water or staying on the deck and fighting the heat. Bonnie was with the group under the water. Liz encouraged me to try it, "So far I've had no accidents on these excursions over the past five years," she added. I pretended that I did not hear her. For a moment the silence spread around us.

The sun was roasting my knees, face and shoulders. I was only wearing a swimsuit and I deeply regretted that I did not bring a hat and overalls. I could not sit on the deck. I absolutely did not have a choice, either I swam around the boat to cool down or went down to the bottom for a walk with the instructor. Liz was staying with me on the deck. "Hold my two hands tight all the time and you will not have any problems." I decided to go down to the bottom with her and she was exhilarated by my decision and she held my two hands tight. "See, not bad, one step at a time and one step and one step," she continuously encouraged me.

Controlling my shaking feet, I put one foot of the first top step and then put my other foot on the same spot. The lukewarm ocean water touched my toes and ankles. It was so good. It felt cool. "Good job. Don't rush. Go slowly," she murmured.

Without saying anything, I put my foot on the second step from the top and the same way as the first one, with the instructor still holding my two hands. "You are doing very well, slowly, slowly. We have seven more steps."

Water came to my knees and waist and shoulders and finally I was under the water. "Not bad at all. Thank you." I finally admitted to her. Strangely enough, I did not feel the weight of the helmet. It was just like I was walking in a deep swimming pool, even though it was fifteen feet under water.

This location under the sea was designated a walking station and had about a fifty yard radius. I saw Kwang and our group and immediately grabbed his hands and let Liz go. The scenery was just like our garden or flowerbed. Rocks and boulders were scattered around. Seaweed was dancing with the waves over the rocks. It was a hilarious, exciting experience. Liz and Bonnie spread the food for the fish and the colorful tropical fish gathered around Kwang's and my helmets. They were not big, four or five inches with long, yellow and black stripes, dark blue, red, blue, with beautiful primitive colors.

The scenery was absolutely breathtaking. We walked around the rocks and the fish were just following us looking for food.

A sting ray with a long tail passed just left of my feet. He scrawled just over the sand. I almost stepped on his long tail. "Uh oh." I screamed. *There might be sharks around us too, because of the vicinity of the sting ray* I thought. I was frightened by even imagining sharks, but the beautiful tropical fish helped diminish my fear.

The water temperature was cool walking on the sand among the rocks, and I was confused about whether I was walking in a garden on the ground or under the sea. Because we were only ten to fifteen feet below the surface, unfortunately, we could not observe the unnamed deep-sea flora and fauna, like Jacques or Jean-Michel Cousteau, but owing to today's technological development, I was having an incredible experience.

About fifty years ago, when I was in high school, I had a dream of wishing for a house under the sea. It was just a dream that under the sea we might design a most beautiful garden and house. That was not just a dream. It is an achievable reality through modern technology.

Walking under the sea was not difficult. It was a little awkward to change steps, no different at all from walking in a swimming pool. Bubbles and fish were floating around my helmet. Everyone was having a hilarious time with a little bouncing of our bodies over the sand. "It is great! A wonderful experience," I told Bonnie. She indicated with bubbles, "I am glad you are having a good time."

Kwang took several pictures with a waterproof camera and still held my hand, walking around the designated territory. Unfortunately, our time was up. About one hour was the maximum for our oxygen tanks. If I did not come down I might have missed astonishing scenery and a once in a lifetime experience.

Figure 102 Underwater Walking

Figure 103   Underwater in Tahiti

Sleeping in a Hammock in Venezuela

In February 2008, we arrived at Caracas, the capital of Venezuela, to see the world famous Tepuis and the highest falls in the world, Angel Falls. Also, the Tepuis was listed as one of the 50 places to see in your lifetime in the National Geographic magazine a decade ago.

Slums surrounded the city with a traffic jam and accidents in several locations, involving trucks turned over carrying steel coils and vegetables on the highway from the airport to our hotel downtown. This left an unfavorable impression of Venezuela. Cabbage and tomato refuse was all over the highway.

The hotel was rated between a two and three star hotel, and a security guard with a gun at his hip stood in front of a steel gate at the hotel's front gate. Everything scared me. *Why did I come here?* I asked myself, but didn't say anything to Kwang, who had worked for a long time to find the right travel agency for this trip. Not many travel agents offer trips to Venezuela, and it was no wonder, based on what I had seen so far.

A small lobby was attached to the dining area and a couple of vinyl sofas were provided. We had to wait until 1:00 p.m. before going to our room after they cleaned it. It was around 10:00 a.m. and the tropical heat and humidity were already hitting us. We could not stay in the lobby where only one fan rotated. We went out onto the street to kill time, strolling on the sidewalk. The shops were closed and locked with big steel gates and heavy locks.

The next morning in a small Cessna four seat passenger airplane we headed out to Canaima National Park where Angel Falls is located. The waterfall drops over the edge of the Auyantepuy Mountain. The plane flew among the dense fog, above the thick tropical jungle, as thick as pea soup. The worst part of it was that we could smell gasoline inside the airplane. Nobody talked, just prayed in my mind for a safe journey without the airplane blowing up. Occasionally the clouds and fog dissipated. Kwang took pictures above Tepuis, which rises in the air like flat tables with the thick jungle below us. He was pretending that there was nothing to be concerned about the gasoline smell.

I kept asking myself, *Why?* *Why am I taking this tremendous risk?* Then I gave myself the same answer. *This is one of the Fifty places to visit in my lifetime. There are only a few more to go. I have to see this one. So, don't complain, please. Just let it go. Everything is going to be fine.*

After two hours of grinding metallic noise from the engine and the overpowering smell of gasoline, the plane landed safely at the Canaima Airport, located near the Carrao River.

"Whoo! Whoo! We made it!" Everybody began talking at once after so much tension. But nobody talked about the extremely dangerous journey.

Already thirty to fifty people were waiting for a boat ride to Angel Falls or a trip back to the capital city of Caracas. Group by group they sat on the ground or on small benches, if they were able to find a seat. Our group was a total of five, including me and my husband, a young man from Holland, a lady from Germany and a middle aged lady from England who sold her house and traveled for one whole year. Her trip to Venezuela was about one-half of the year's journey. The rest of the year she would travel in Asia, China, Vietnam and Thailand. They were the same age as our children. I was envious that they were able to travel one month or one year at their young age without concerns about job security. When we were their age we were busy settling down in our careers. Anyway, Kwang and I had to stick together with these young people for the next twelve days without becoming a burden. The man from Holland asked me, "Your children do not like to travel?" "Yes, they do but they are busy working". I did not tell him, but I wanted to add, "In the USA, if you take two weeks vacation, your desk may be gone. Our children are busy holding their jobs and building their careers". I remembered the story in Europe. "Four days per week are workdays and at least one month vacation in the summer." I was not sure if this was true or not, but it is different from the U.S.A.

It was around noon and already the motorized canoe was ready for us at the riverbank. More people joined us and two boatmen in long, narrow canoes. All twelve of us were on board wearing orange life jackets with lots of brown stains. Two sat side by side and the canoe had seven or eight rows.

The canoe began maneuvering against the stream. It was absolutely beautiful scenery. The crystal clear water was deep enough that the canoe could pass many narrow streams for two hours. I put my hands into the water and cooled my body temperature down through my hands. Green moss was hanging from the trees like drapery, competing for the place with hummingbirds that were flying from tree to tree.

But now the water became shallow and rocks and boulders prevented us from going further upstream. Several times, the canoe operators and the male passengers jumped into the knee-high water and pushed the canoe to get it to move.

At first the small space in the canoe was tolerable for my butt, but after three or four hours on the wooden bench my threshold of tolerance was gone and I used my life jacket as a cushion. The sunlight was getting hotter and I hoped suntan lotion would help against sunburn. I was getting very tired and thirsty. Again, the images of the beautiful scenery disappeared and I looked for comfortable ways to travel. I was totally exhausted.

I chose this, I said to myself. *It's nobody else's fault. I just have to be careful of what I eat and where I sleep.* I had left the word "comfort" behind at home.

Now, for a couple of miles, the canoe passed dark green bottom and then we came to almost the color of dark blood, a red bottom area. The guide told us it is Jasper stone which is reddish with black stripes in the middle and makes a beautiful mosaic design. The leaves from the tropical trees fall in the river for a thousand years and it becomes a beautiful reddish color. Jasper is a semi-precious gemstone like amber in the Black Sea.

Now the water was even shallower, covered with small gravel. The blade of the motor had worn out and was replaced with a new one. Of course, several times during our six-hour trip to the bottom of Angel Falls we pushed the canoe through shallow areas. Finally we came to a small creek. Both sides had big picnic shelters with a roof, no windows, no walls and only a cement floor. It was around 7:00 p.m. but it was not dark yet. The sun was still in the sky, making it pleasant and welcoming us to our final destination of the day.

For our evening meal, they served a unique barbecue chicken breast that was hung like Jacob's ladder around the huge campfire. The dinner was set up on a long table for our twelve people and twenty more people from another group joined us later. Cafeteria style, or like in the army, we lined up with paper plates for chicken, corn, bread and soda. The dinner was one of the best chicken breasts I ever had with large ears of sweet corn. This corn was a special species in South America.

When we started to have dinner the sun was down and it became chilly and dark shadows surrounded us. While we were having dinner the guides quickly set up about forty – forty five white hammocks in the shelter. Each hammock was separated by only about one meter distance. As the sun went down, the invasion of an army of mosquitoes was more difficult to tolerate than the tropical heat and thirst.

They put candles at few meters intervals on the poles between the white hammocks with mosquito nets. Only one thin blanket was provided. I wore everything I brought, sweater, jeans and socks to overcome the chilly air. About three rows, ten - fifteen hammocks in each row, were hung for about forty people. I was almost in the middle of the outside toward the mountainside.

The full moon was starting to rise over the mountaintop and the guides set out candles. The hammocks were ready and they were our only option. Otherwise we had no chance of winning the battle against the mosquitoes. It was the first time I slept in a hammock. I always thought that people in hammocks under trees were extremely lazy people, or a poet and a writer who was lost for an idea of what to write. In this case the hammock was above a cement floor, not green grass and not under trees.

"Here is a flashlight." Kwang gave me a small pocket flashlight in case of an emergency. "How about you?" was my question. "I have the same one you have and I brought an extra battery, too." Kwang was on my left side and another heavy guy was on my right. It was getting dark and I could not see his face clearly. Anyway, he did not belong as a member of my "five member" group.

After about five minutes of pouring tropical rain, luckily the full moon returned. I could not sleep. The men as well as ladies started snoring like an orchestra concert. With all the continuous snoring and heavy breathing sounds and the noise of the mosquitoes, I could not sleep. "Whang, whang, whang," above my net and so, I could not sleep.

Why am I so stupid? Most of my friends, I mean wives, if they do not like what their husbands are suggesting, just say "No. Period". They do not blindly obey their husband. *Why am I doing this?* I am just looking up at the ceiling of the roof sheltering us.

Somehow I fell asleep but I needed to go to the restroom in the middle of the night which was far away from the shelter. Under the full moon it was not too bad finding my way to the natural bathroom bush. After my business was done, I put my head in the opposite direction from where I could see the mountain and at least part of the sky. The snoring from the other people was diminishing, a little better than before.

I have to get some sleep, then I can climb up to the bottom of Angel Falls. I was told it is very tough. I spoke to myself.

When I woke up it was dawn. Some people were already up and making whistling and humming sounds. The blanket helped me avoid the cold. It was a chilly morning. The clean air almost made me forget last night's adventure in the hammock.

229

After about four hours of climbing through the extremely slippery road because of the rain the night before, and through the obstacles of tangled and twisted tree roots and boulders, we arrived at Angel Falls which is about fifty – seventy yards away from the actual bottom.

February is the dry season of the year. The water falls down like white shoestrings from the Tepuis (flat rock mountain). Looking from a far distance, I thought the immense amount of water was falling down from the mountain, but the long water string from Tepuis is just like a post card scene, "thin thread".

From our location when we looked down at the bottom of the falls, water drops made dense fog and we had to wear raincoats. Kwang used a waterproof camera. The water falls down over one thousand meters making for a foggy environment at the bottom.

It is spectacular and an absolutely stunning view. The power of the wonders of nature astonished me. But, honestly I was disappointed that the volume of water was extremely low, quite a contrast to Niagara Falls and Iguazu Falls, on the basis of the volume of the water.

I was told that in the rainy season the amount of water from Angel Falls is an unbelievable volume. Maybe that's true, if water was not shallow to come here, the propeller had not been grinding up, guides and men did not need to jump into the water and push the boat.

This is true everywhere in Venezuela? We can see small and large falls and Tepuis along with abundant oil resources. Angel Falls did not meet our expectations, but some in our group were pleased. Coming down from the falls was more challenging through the extremely slippery green moss covered boulders, and the roots of trees were indescribably hazardous and tangled on the trail. When we came back to our shelter it was late afternoon. I was delighted that the scene of hammocks hanging on the ceiling was gone. I could not sleep another night inside a hammock with such a large group of people.

The next stop was the Orinoco Delta area through the countless branching of canals and unnamed tropical plants, and flowers and a fence of mangrove trees on the river banks. The motorboats cruised up and down the Orinoco River and up to the nearby Shell Oil exploring platform connected to the Atlantic Ocean.

Occasionally you can see a residential area, one or two houses on the river bank. The houses have only palm leaf roofs and floors of three - four meters above the ground and there were no walls and windows, just open walls. The kitchen is in the middle of the floor with a campfire for the cooking of food. At the north side of the corners, there were two empty hammocks hanging on a pole waiting for somebody to sleep or relax in it. Four ladies and two men were making baskets and plates from palm leaves. The beautiful design created one of the masterpieces in the jungle. Without a second thought as to whether they were expensive or a reasonable price, I bought one plate and two baskets for my daughter and daughters-in-law. The man showed us a hammock for sale. It was very intricate and strung from palm leaves. The young man from Holland was negotiating from thirty dollars to twenty dollars, I heard. Even thirty dollars is one third of the price in the USA. Whatever price it might be, I hated sleeping in a hammock. I will not dream again of reading a book in a hammock under the Maple tree in summer while peacefully watching squirrels running around and butterflies flying around my hammock, not fighting mosquitoes. The young man from the Netherlands did not buy it. Maybe he had the same memories of struggling and fighting with mosquitoes and the snoring in the hammock last night.

The boat stopped in the dense jungle. There was an abundant variety of fruits, cocoa, bananas and others. As we walked through the jungle, he showed us how to get fresh water from tree leaves, make hats from plants and play like Tarzan, swinging from tree to tree. I used all the force of my arms and legs to swing my body on the tree branches from one to another as the guide had showed us. It involved principles of physics and the right timing and movements to exercise the force of my arms and legs. It was quite fun. Kwang and our group members were happy that I started to enjoy my trip. Before, I was grumpy about mosquito attacks, hard climbing to the bottom of Angel Falls and the disappointment of the Falls being like spaghetti strips. Kwang made a hat for me to cheer me up. I wore it for a couple of hours.

In the jungle lots of swamps were scattered around. That's why they provided knee high rubber boots. When we were crossing swamps on the very narrow logs I lost my balance and fell into the swamp. One half of my body was covered in mud. Luckily my face was untouched. Also, luckily that spot was almost the last spot near our shelter for the night's stay. Instead of embarrassment, I was really scared about the snakes in the mud. It was hard to get me out of the swamp. Two men were not enough to pull me out, as though it was quicksand. I cleaned up at the riverbank where there were several stairs to the main shelter. The feeling was awesome, jumping into the clean and cool Orinoco River after a couple of hours of jungle walk and getting covered with mud. This shelter was more upgraded than the previous one near Angel Falls, because a quite clean bathroom was available, even if it was a primitive one hole facility, and the floor was not cement. It was made of logs with small gaps in between.

We had a candlelight dinner with fish from the river. Under the full moon, if the mosquitoes were not there, it would have been a very romantic place. On the bank of the river there was a beautiful shelter and tropical plants behind. Unknown birds were chirping and monkeys were swinging from tree to tree making loud noises and looking for mates. But, after sunset, as it was getting dark, the wild group of mosquitoes invaded and attacked us, even though we continuously sprayed ourselves with mosquito repellant, and we had to give up sitting on the bench with beer and coffee.

I was inside the hammock again. It was not bad like the first hammock because our group was just five, but my problems did not go away. After sunset it was getting rather cold. I asked for a blanket. No supply of blankets. Kwang was upset. "You are not special. You are asking too much!" I did not ask for anything special, just a blanket. I was almost crying and I felt like pushing him into the river. I wore everything I had with me, two pants with jeans and turtleneck and a sweater with a hood I brought along, just in case. It was tropical temperature in the daytime, but at night it was not quite arctic, but it was cold. Even after a cold night, in the morning the mosquito attacks never ended.

Angel Falls is a magnificent example of God's handiwork and a thrilling natural wonder. I am glad I visited there and finished an unusual and difficult journey sleeping in a hammock surrounded by flocks of mosquitoes.

Figure 104 Pushing Canoe

Figure 105   Hammock

Figure 106   Hammock Camp

Figure 107   Hammock Hut

Figure 108   Angel Falls

Figure 109 Angel Falls, 1000 meter drop

The Red Boat, Explorer

On November 23, 2007, Kwang told me CNN News said that the Red Boat "Explorer" was sunk near Antarctica's South Shetland Islands, between Ushuaia, Argentina and Antarctic Peninsula. Fortunately, all one hundred fifty four crew members and the guests were safely rescued. The accident occurred predawn Friday morning. Struck by submerged ice, the entire vessel finally slipped beneath the waves on Friday evening after a twenty hour struggle, pumping out water from the boat. Pumping out the water was ineffective in saving the Red Boat, because the fist sized hole in the side of the hull was too big.

The group of one hundred fifty four people calmly abandoned the ship when the captain's order came and pumping water out of the ship helped to keep the Red Boat stable for an orderly evacuation.

The Norwegian Lines, Nordnorge ferried the passengers and the crew to a Chilean air force base on King George Island in Antarctic waters near southernmost South America

"Woo, Woo. Everyone was safe," I said.

"Kwang, but the Red Boat was beautiful and efficient."

He agreed.

"But the Red Boat was sunk. That's my favorite boat and I plan to write a story about our Antarctica trip with the Red Boat "Explorer". It was hard to hide my emotional attachment to this Red Boat.

The Red Boat "Explorer" is owned by G.A.P. (Great Adventures People) Adventures of Toronto, Ontario, Canada. G.A.P. is a tour company that provides excursions with an environmental focus. It provides the tour for a nineteen day circuit of Antarctica and the Falkland Islands, letting passengers observe penguins, whales and other wildlife while getting briefings from experts on the region on the Red Boat.

In January 2005 we planned to take a trip to Antarctica with G.A.P. Adventures, but on January 13, 2005 I had a terrible car accident in Kokomo, Indiana. Our trip to Antarctica was postponed until December 2005.

We arrived at Ushuia, Argentina from Atlanta, Georgia, in the early morning in order to start the cruise of the Antarctic Peninsula with the Red Boat in the afternoon. The cruise started at 3:00 p.m. We had time to stroll around downtown Ushuia which has only two streets with souvenir shops and restaurants. Almost every item in the shop was related to penguins, key chains, stuffed ones and postcards.

The unusual lists of items that G.A.P. suggested we had to bring for this trip was two pairs of wool gloves and socks and knee-high rubber boots with good warm liners, and of course, turtlenecks and sweaters and waterproof warm coat and pants. As usual, Kwang prepared well for this unique trip with all the necessary gear.

For no special reason, I fell in love with the Red Boat as soon as I was on board. There were only one hundred passengers and about fifty total crew members and managers on the boat. Not really small, not really huge. Ordinarily an ocean liner holds about three thousand people.

The white color of the boat is normal on the ocean. This red boat has a red colored stripe in the middle of the body of the boat. That's where the nickname "Red Boat" came from.

After a couple of hours delay waiting for several passengers the Red Boat left from Ushuia to the Antarctic Peninsula. We could see nothing, only endless azure color of the sky and water was spreading along the big icebergs, floating far away from the boat. But the white seagulls were around the master of the boat and they stayed with it.

During two days' and nights' journey crossing Drake Passage to the Antarctic Peninsula, humpback whales were scratching their bodies against the boat and then blowing water out, as photogenic creatures, and sea lions took naps on the icebergs. Meanwhile, inside the boat, we watched the movie, "March of the Penguins" and had lectures about whales, sea lions and animals and plants in Antarctica provided by retired experts.

The shape of the icebergs were magic kingdoms, big castles, lions, flat mountains, tall poles. It was a stunning view. Their colors were changing from white to deep blue under the reflection of the sun. It was just like a modern abstract picture, much better than Picasso.

We landed on several islands and peninsulas. Whenever we had an excursion on icy land, we had to sanitize our rubber boots from the Red Boat to Jodiak and also before stepping on land again we had to clean our boots with a brush that was already provided.

There are several research centers from different countries, such as the United States, Russia, United Kingdom, Korea, Japan, China and Argentina. They open the research center for about five months in the summer. December was a little bit early to open many research centers. Only the Ukrainian Center was available.

Through a narrow snow bank making a tunnel, we arrived at the Ukrainian Research Center. At a glance I could see that only men scientists are living in this building. Lots of pictures of women in bikinis were on the wall.

Some souvenirs from the Ukraine were for sale and some science fiction books were on the shelf. Strong coffee and vodka were available for purchase. Six months during the wintertime it is closed and six months in summertime it is open, from November to May. Most of the people are working here for two or three years for advanced research related to Antarctica. There are several rooms for special data collections, such as temperature and humidity variations and other important data for military purposes. After a quick tour they served us strong European coffee and vodka for purchase.

We got our visa for Antarctica stamped and also we can mail postcards from here to the USA. I sent several cards with extra expensive stamps. At that moment I did not know my postcards first go to the Ukraine and from the Ukraine to the USA. The cards we mailed to the U.S. arrived six months after we finished our trip.

"Antarctica means penguins, or penguins mean Antarctica?" Kwang asked. "Yes, they are everywhere," I added.

They are all over the snowy hills, icebergs and in the water. They are always marching in groups and following the leader. Whenever an urgent and unique signal is sent to the leader about fifteen to twenty penguins slide down a snowy hill and jump into the icy water. A couple of penguins hesitated before going in the water and then later they all jumped in the water. We clapped for them.

"Just like the movie, 'March of Penguins," I told Kwang. He watched the amazing phenomena of penguin activities. We were both speechless.

In the water they performed gymnastics and hid under the ice slabs and came out on the snow bank, flapping their wings to get rid of all the water on their bodies and marching back up the white hill. Another group came down and they took almost the same route. The penguins were not afraid of us. We walked alongside the penguins, like holding a baby's hands. Even though they waddled, they moved faster than we did because our feet were immersed in the deep snow, but they slid down. While looking at their greasy soft feathers, it was hard to restrain the temptation to touch them and hold them.

You may think that Antarctica only has ice and snow on the land, but we saw several places with gray ground with gravel. On this gray ground the penguins made nests with gravel, which were two feet diameter on the ground and formed a fence. When we arrived on the land and passed just nearby the nest side, they did not move. I was told for nesting not only female, but also male penguins take turns and sit over the eggs. Usually one egg, but sometimes two eggs. We saw a brown baby chick come out from the mother. Strangely, baby chicks are brown color and later, when they are grown up, turn into a beautiful white and black color with greasy, glistening velvet type feathers. The penguins that are not nesting are protecting the penguins that have nests. They work together as a team.

The stunning views of the penguins on each island were breathtaking, but cruising among the small icebergs with the Jodiak after the Red Boat docked at the icy shore, or icy land. It was a fantastic moment when the boat was through the small icy channel. It reminded me of scenes of the Titanic's death throes, where it was against the mammoth iceberg like a white mosaic on the sea.

On another occasion the captain woke us up after dinner, almost 10:00 p.m. for another landing on the ice. Red Boat pushed into icy land and the GAP director and a couple of engineers checked the thickness of the ice to see if we could land on the ice to reach the island without the Jodiak. It was quite a unique experience, walking on the ice. The captain docked the Red Boat just on the ice ... mysteriously touched the ice. Instructions were only ten people at a time. At first we were very careful, walking cautiously on the ice, but after a couple of steps we walked on the ice to the peninsula.

"What an experience, walking on the ice in Antarctica," I told Kwang. He nodded.

We walked around the icy and snowy island for about twenty minutes. I saw the Red Boat "our boat" standing by in the distance against the white world.

With these experiences in Antarctica, Red Boat, penguins and their nests on gravel, snowy hills, icebergs and Reserch and Development centers, I cannot believe that the Red Boat sank into the ocean, even though she collided with a thousand, thousand icebergs.

Figure 110 Pushing Through Ice Field

Figure 111   Red Boat

Figure 112   Red Boat

Figure 113   Penguins

Figure 114 Humpback Whale

Figure 115   Antarctic Iceberg

Figure 116 Antarctic Iceberg

Figure 117   Penguins feeding Baby

Figure 118   Walking on Ice

Figure 119   Red Boat

Restaurant on Island

We spent a night in a small fishing village in Paraty, in Brazil. It was quite comfortable sleeping compared to Rio de Janeiro which has sticky humidity. Also the loud tropical birds, macaws and others, did not wake us up.

Today is a very easy day, starting with a late breakfast and then going to a fish market. The breakfast was just toast, coffee and Chiquita bananas. It is too simple. I would like to have at least one boiled egg for breakfast. Nobody had any complaints, so I should be satisfied. Carlos, our guide, came and talked about good Brazilian coffee so good it's sold to Starbucks. He did not mention anything about our cheap unbalanced breakfast but indicated "Wait. A nice lunch is waiting for you."

After walking into the village along one mile on the gravel road, we came upon a main street with small jewelry and souvenir shops. It was too early in the morning and the stores were all closed. *Oh, well, I will be back* I murmured in my mind.

On the shore, fish markets were open, carrying some vegetables and fruits. Green onions and cucumbers were in the baskets for sale, but they were not fresh and were ready to be thrown into the trash. We strolled along the shore for ten - fifteen minutes waiting for our boat to arrive, but there wasn't much beach to enjoy.

The boat was a double-decker with capacity for about forty people, and it cruised out a couple of miles from the shore in Paraty to a small sand beach. The boat docked in the middle of the sea twenty yards away from the beach. Then we swam around the boat and dove from the deck into the water.

The hot tropical sun was scorching and swimming in Paraty Bay was kind of a luxury in mid-December, compared to fighting cold and snow in Detroit. Carlos and a couple of younger people swam like dolphins, without a care in the world.

A couple of yards away from the beach, in a tropical rain forest, Carlos found a poisonous frog with a greenish body and red dots. It was very small, about the size of a big man's thumb. I thought this frog has a great survival device in the forest.

It was almost noon and we enjoyed a couple of hours in the water. Next we toured around the coast of the Paraty Bay through the canals with mangrove trees among the small islands.

We were starving by this time and Carlos found a restaurant on a tiny island, "Eh Laho Bar e Restaurante". Our double decker could not reach the island because of the shallow water, so a tanned man, mid-thirties, with curly hair, took us ashore in his motorboat.

Carlos repeated that he would treat us to the most exclusive restaurant in the world, at least in Paraty, Brazil. "For lunch it is not easy to make a reservation. It has to be made two - three months ahead of time." He had tried to do his best for us, such as this restaurant and the powerful and expensive Swarovski telescope from which we could see objects clearly and took pictures by attaching our digital camera to the telescope.

When we arrived at the dining area in the corner of the restaurant, one couple was at the table with casual conversation over a Margarita and whiskey sour. Only two tables for four people along the north side of the dining area, long table in the middle for a large group and east side against the wall of the kitchen, three tables for four people each ready for guests. That's all they have, the tables and chairs are made of wood, one level higher class than picnic tables. Maybe the total area is one thousand to one thousand five hundred square feet. The restaurant is built on four - five huge boulders connected with wooden floors and no windows, just open space. The boulders are at least ten feet wide and fifteen feet high. The roof is thatched with banana leaves. The structure is very primitive but I can feel somewhat unique cultural and elegant atmosphere. There are no other islands out here in the middle of nowhere. Just like a seagull drops from the sky, make this island. The surroundings are quiet. No motorboats, sailboats and there aren't even any fishing boats. Just the sea and the restaurant. I could say "wow", different, unique and I wish I could have this kind of island in my life.

There is a tiny bar in the northwest corner with a wooden counter which can hold five - six glasses. The wine and hard liquor glasses are dangling from the ceiling under the thatched roof. The kitchen area is one house (I could say, instead of building) and the bar area is another small house attached to the boulders. Between these two houses white beach umbrellas are open for shade.

Our group, a total of twelve people, sat at the long table for a late lunch. As usual I provided a box lunch for Kwang and myself from the hotel with Chiquita bananas and tomatoes, sausage links in a can and a small roll to avoid eating too much greasy food from the restaurant.

We all wandered around the dining area. The floor is about less than two feet above water level and the tropical fish are swimming around hunting for food falling from the tables. They are beautiful, yellow, red, white and black and white stripes. They are not big, just the size of my hands. We were all tempted to jump into the water.

The east side kitchen is the only place that is not open to the sea. On every side you can see the beautiful water with small white waves with the strong tropical sunlight making it more silver-white. Occasionally sea gulls were diving into the water to catch fish. This is a small piece of Heaven surrounded between blue sky and water.

How in the world boulders were gathered this way and used to construct a house and restaurant! After we passed the kitchen, a couple of yards away from the dining area, there is a generator room on the east side from the main dining area. Small rocks scattered around the area make it narrower than the dining area and further south was a tiny island connected to the restaurant by a seven - eight yards long swing bridge.

Every corner and hole on the rocks have unknown cacti and plants are blooming under the blue sky like mosaics. On the left there is a narrow wooden passage among the rocks leading to the dock where a small rowboat was tied to the right and there was a tiny beach with shallow water. Mom and baby, maybe six months old, were enjoying a small natural swimming pool in the middle of the ocean. The woman wore a beautiful bikini and seemed not to be shy without covering anything on her body.

"Hello" I started. "Hello" back to me with an accent. "It is so beautiful here", I continued. "Yes" her answer was short. "I think you are the owner?" I expected her answer was "yes".

"Yes." My husband and I have owned the restaurant for seven years" then she continued with an accent and was glad to tell the story.

When they were students from the Netherlands visiting to study biological aspects for three months they fell in love with the geological and biological phenomena in Brazil and they came back for further study.

The fascinating weather, breathtaking scenery like Serra de Bocaina Mountains, and specific species can be found only in Brazil, such as huge blue butterflies, giant lizard, snails, crocodiles, birds. It is paradise for scientists, like the Galapagos Islands for Darwin. She and her husband decided to settle down in Brazil and bought this island (I cannot say island. It is a group of boulders, as I said before) and opened the restaurant. All the designs came from her husband. They had more business than they could handle and had to make reservations a couple of months ahead. "What about dinner?" I interrupted her.

"A reservation for dinner is more difficult. We have a total of forty seats available." "Yum" I sighed.

"Under the moonlight and listening to the waves and the shadow of the moon makes it more romantic. Most couples want to celebrate their anniversaries and wives' birthdays on this island."

I nodded and she asked me "Where do you come from?" "America." She did not expect me to answer that I come from the

USA. "Originally?" "Oh. From Korea," I continued "From South Korea."

The baby was not happy in the water any more. It was time for a nap. We exchanged "goodbyes". Then she went toward her house and Kwang and I followed her to the small island across the swinging bridge connected to the restaurant. The island is a residential area and has both big and small trees like a regular island. On a large tree branch a small swing set is hanging. It seemed she has another older child besides the baby.

On the right hand side near the bar there is a small picnic area with a small grill and table for four people. This is a good place that we can have our lunch. Instead of sitting down for lunch we strolled more until we could not enter the residential area any more.

At the front a white puppy lay down for a nap. Everything was so quiet.

At the picnic table we had our lunch dreaming … were we in Heaven or in the real world. The crystal clear water touched the shore and left white bubbles on the sand.

Our group was still waiting for their lunch. Preparing lunch for just twelve people took about one hour. Did they intentionally take a long time in order for the guests to enjoy the scenery? "You picked the right spot to have a picnic. There is no other spot better than this" one of our group members commented. "We are still waiting for our food" the old men complained. *We cannot have an experience like this any other place. Let's enjoy it as long as we can stay* I did not tell him but murmured.

Kwang took pictures of the restaurant from many angles … close ups and from a distance. He seemed to hate the idea of leaving.

Figure 120   Island Restaurant